ADMINISTRATIVE MANAGEMENT
CASE STUDIES

RUNSHAW COLLEGE
LIBRARY
LEYLAND

Books are to be returned on or before the last date below.

RUNSHAW COLLEGE
025422

ADMINISTRATIVE MANAGEMENT CASE STUDIES

Maureen Haddow

Pitman

PITMAN PUBLISHING
128 Long Acre, London WC2E 9AN

A Division of Longman Group UK Limited

© Longman Group UK Limited 1992

First published in Great Britain 1992

British Library Cataloguing-in-Publication Data
A catalogue record for this book is available from the British Library

ISBN 0-273-03812-5

All rights reserved; no part of this publication may
be reproduced, stored in a retrieval system, or
transmitted in any form or by any means, electronic,
mechanical, photocopying, recording or otherwise
without either the prior written permission of the
Publishers or a licence permitting restricted copying
in the United Kingdom issued by the Copyright Licensing
Agency Ltd, 90 Tottenham Court Road, London W1P 9HE.
This book may not be lent, resold, hired out or otherwise
disposed of by way of trade in any form of binding or
cover other than that in which it is published, without
the prior consent of the Publishers.

Printed and bound in Great Britain

Contents

Preface vii

Acknowledgements ix

List of skills developed x

1 INTRODUCTION 1

    1.1 The case study - note to tutors 2
    1.2 Guidelines for approaching a case study 4
    1.3 Specimen case study 7

2 ORGANISATIONAL STRUCTURE AND PRINCIPLES 17

    2.1 Centralisation and decentralisation 18
    2.2 Organisational relationships 21
    2.3 Delegation 24

3 EFFECTIVE COMMUNICATION 29

    3.1 Barriers to communication 30
    3.2 Report-writing 34
    3.3 Telephone techniques 38

4 GENERAL ADMINISTRATIVE PROCEDURES AND PUBLIC RELATIONS 43

    4.1 Reception 45
    4.2 Appointments and diary management 48
    4.3 Time management, working relationships and administrative procedures 51
    4.4 Travel arrangements 54

5 INFORMATION MANAGEMENT 59

    5.1 Records management 61
    5.2 Records management and general administrative procedures 64
    5.3 Business documentation 67
    5.4 Statistical presentation 69

6 MEETINGS 73

    6.1 Preparation for meetings 74
    6.2 Effective meetings 78
    6.3 Effective minutes (1) 82
    6.4 Effective minutes (2) 86

    6.5 Effective minutes (3) 88
    6.6 Meetings role-play 91

7 THE INDIVIDUAL WITHIN THE ORGANISATION 101

    7.1 Manpower planning 102
    7.2 Recruitment 105
    7.3 Selection interviewing 107

8 MANAGING CHANGE 111

    8.1 Planning change 112
    8.2 Planning and managing change 115
    8.3 Overcoming resistance to change 119
    8.4 Training 122
    8.5 Job design 125
    8.6 Job evaluation 129
    8.7 Ergonomics, health and safety 135
    8.8 Negotiation role-play exercise 139

9 INTEGRATED CASES 143

    9.1 General administrative systems 144
    9.2 In-tray exercise 148
    9.3 Management of change 160

10 TUTOR GUIDELINES 165

    10.1 Suggestions for the management of case study sessions 166
    10.2 Suggestions for the management of role-play sessions 168
    10.3 Assessing group case studies and role-play exercises 171
    10.4 Writing a case study or role-play exercise 174

Preface

Administrative Management incorporates a series of case studies which are designed to provide a useful training vehicle for those studying the management of the administrative function on a wide range of full-time and part-time courses. The book will be particularly useful for those studying for NVQ and SVQ levels 3 and 4, BTEC and SCOTVEC Higher National Diploma level and equatable examinations of City and Guilds, RSA and similar examination bodies. The material is also highly appropriate to those studying for SCE Higher Grade or for the Certificate of Sixth Year Studies. In addition, it will be useful for degree students and those attending short courses who are involved in administration within very different types of organisation.

The case studies are based on problems currently experienced by organisations and most of the material is drawn from real life observations and discussions with administrative and managerial staff.

- The book is divided into 10 sections. Section 1 introduces the case study technique, giving some guidelines for students on how to approach a case study and providing a sample case study incorporating guideline answers.

  The following 7 sections are devoted to case studies which centre around specific aspects of administrative management. Each of these sections commences with an introduction, which briefly examines the areas to be covered, relating them to the overall theme of administrative management.

  Section 9 contains integrated case studies which involve a range of problems and encourage the student to apply previously acquired knowledge and skills to the management of complexity.

  The last section provides guidelines for tutors on the management and assessment of case study and role-play sessions as well as guidelines on the writing of a case study.

- The sections are designed to cover the major theoretical concepts and problem areas within administrative management, with emphasis in a number of cases being given to issues related to information technology.

- Since the aim of a case study is to be as realistic as possible, it is seldom feasible to restrict the case to dealing with one aspect only. Students should therefore be encouraged to examine the case study in the light of their complete theoretical knowledge and not merely their knowledge of the stated theme of the case. In this way students will develop their awareness and understanding of the complexity of management and begin to adopt a holistic approach to problem-solving.

- The sections may be studied in sequence or at random and a guide is given to the different skills required within each case.

- Each case has a series of possible ACTIONS at the end, some, or all, of which can be used, depending on the time available and the level of ability of the student.

Acknowledgements

I would like to express my sincere thanks to a number of people who have helped me in the production of this book. Members of staff and, in particular, the technician staff from the Department of Business Information Management, Napier Polytechnic, gave most generously of their time to advise and support me. Feedback from students and colleagues who piloted the case studies was particularly helpful as was the friendly help from staff at Pitman. The support and encouragement from friends and family, particularly my parents who reviewed sections of the text and saw less of me than usual, was invaluable. Finally, special thanks are due to Betsy Stevenson who spent many hours reviewing and proofreading the material and whose very valuable comments were much appreciated.

MH

List of skills developed

SKILL	2.1	2.2	2.3	3.1	3.2	3.3	4.1	4.2	4.3	4.4	5.1	5.2	5.3	5.4	6.1	6.2
Analysis	x	x	x	x	x	x	x	x	x	x	x	x	x	x	x	x
Problem solving	x	x	x	x	x	x	x	x	x	x	x	x	x	x	x	x
Decision making	x	x	x	x	x	x	x	x	x	x	x	x	x	x	x	x
Communication (written)	x	x	x		x	x	x	x		x		x				x
Report writing	x	x			x		x									x
Documenting procedures				x	x		x		x			x			x	
Flow-chart design													x			
Organisational chart design		x														
Graph production (manual)														x		
Graph production (electronic)														x		
Spreadsheet design														x		

CASE

CASE

SKILL	6.3	6.4	6.5	6.6	7.1	7.2	7.3	8.1	8.2	8.3	8.4	8.5	8.6	8.7	8.8	9.1	9.2	9.3
Analysis	x	x	x	x	x	x	x	x	x	x	x	x	x	x	x	x	x	x
Problem solving	x				x	x	x		x	x	x	x	x	x	x	x	x	x
Decision making	x	x	x	x	x		x	x	x	x	x	x	x	x	x	x	x	x
Communication (verbal)				x		x		x			x			x			x	x
Communication (written)	x	x	x						x	x	x				x			
Report writing												x				x		
Documenting procedures							x											
Presentation						x					x						x	x
Minute writing	x	x	x	x														
Meeting chairmanship				x														
Minute taking				x														
Negotiation															x			
Time management																	x	
Designing a training programme												x						
Team building												x			x			
Drafting job description						x												
Drafting personnel specification						x												

SECTION 1
INTRODUCTION

The use of case studies has become an integral part of many training programmes. This is particularly true of programmes where the aim is to develop theoretical knowledge which the trainee can then apply in a practical situation.

This section is designed to introduce the trainee to the case study technique by examining the aims and problems associated with the case study method of learning and by providing the trainee with guidelines on how to approach a case study. In order to give further help to the trainee a sample case study is given and a guideline answer provided.

A trainee who has an understanding of the case study technique will be in a better position to learn from the subsequent sections of this book where the case study technique is applied to the area of administrative management.

1.1 The case study - note to tutors

The case study is a vehicle which presents students with an opportunity to apply their learning to the analysis and solving of problems of a real-life or simulated nature. It aids the students' development of real-life skills as well as reinforcing and applying their theoretical knowledge.

Features of a case study

1. A case study enables students to relate theory to practice.

2. It is a method for developing skills in a classroom environment where the students can experiment and learn as there is little at stake as compared with a real business situation.

   These skills include:
   - analytical skills
   - problem-solving skills
   - decision-making skills
   - clear thinking
   - creative skills
   - communication skills
   - interpersonal skills
   - team-building skills
   - self-analysis skills

3. Case studies can provide stimulation to the learning situation by helping the students to see the relevance of the theoretical learning. This is particularly so when students work in groups and when they can relate their own experience to aspects of the case situation.

4. A case study is a vehicle for enabling students to gain an insight into the complexity of real life.

5. It can be used as a method of assessing a student's understanding of different theoretical concepts and their inter-relationship since a mere regurgitation of rote learning is not appropriate.

6. When combined with role play, a case study gives the additional advantage of enabling the students to gain experience of:
   - carrying out the task
   - the challenge and stresses which arise
   - the resulting influence on their behaviour patterns and those of the other players

- the effect of the various behaviour patterns on the development of the exercise.

Problems which can be encountered

For a number of reasons, students, at first, often find this method quite difficult and confusing.

a Students may not be quite clear what they are supposed to be doing or what their goal is. For this reason it is vital that students who are unfamiliar with this vehicle of learning are given guidelines on how to tackle a case study and are closely monitored when working through their first case study.

b The concept that there is often no *one* correct answer may be confusing.

c Students may experience difficulty with the complexities and ambiguities of the case and the usually limited amount of information with which they are provided. Whereas it is vital to give sufficient information, it is worth remembering that too much information can sometimes add to the confusion and that, in real life, work frequently has to be done and decisions made with incomplete information.

d A lack of adequate preparation prior to the case study session can cause problems. Students should be made aware of the importance of preparation and be given every encouragement to undertake this.

e The value of the case study will be reduced if, at the end of the exercise, there is uncertainty over what has been learned or whether in fact anything of value has been learned. The situation can be complicated if they do not realise that it is often a skill which is being developed rather than a series of facts being learned. The debriefing session should be used to overcome such confusion.

f Students can experience problems because of an apparent lack of leadership by the tutor who is encouraging the students to define and take responsibility for their own learning rather than adopting the more traditional role of teaching or lecturing. Careful preparation of the students prior to undertaking case studies should help to obviate this confusion.

Regardless of these difficulties, however, and with due attention having been given to reducing and overcoming them, the case study technique is a very valuable and rewarding instrument of learning.

1.2 Guidelines for approaching a case study

1 Introduction and overview

Read the case study through fairly quickly in order to gain an overall appreciation of the situation and problem. On the first reading do not stop to try to clarify anything which is not immediately clear.

2 Identify what is required of you

Read carefully what you are expected to do (ie study the questions or instructions at the end of the case). Examine in detail the wording of these instructions to ensure that you have fully understood what it is you are being asked to do. For example, are you being asked to carry out a general analysis, to make general recommendations or are you being asked to be much more specific and produce a practical and detailed action plan and/or carry out a role-play.

3 Second reading and examination

Re-read the case slowly making sure that you understand each section. During the reading it is recommended that you underline key words and phrases and make notes in the margin as this will ease subsequent identification and analysis of the case study. The use of numbering or lettering in the margin will be of considerable assistance at a later stage when you are trying to identify any relationship between points or issues.

Look for any hidden meaning or information in the case as well as obvious information, but be careful not to jump too quickly to conclusions, which may be incorrect.

Recognise that information on people's past behaviour and attitudes can give clues to their present and future behaviour. When providing an answer to the case, anticipated reactions and behaviour must be taken into consideration.

4 Identify and distinguish facts and opinions

Facts can be exact, vague, general or rather doubtful. It is important that you can identify the category into which they fall.

Opinions should be recognised for what they are - they may be valid or invalid. Regardless of their validity, however, they must be considered because they are likely to influence the behaviour and attitude of those who hold them.

5 Examine and question your findings

Learn to question the meaning of facts and attempt to identify possible messages from them. Always remember that you may be given extraneous material to test your ability to sift out the facts efficiently.

6 Organise the information

At this stage it is important to organise the information under appropriate headings. This will aid the analysis of the case by highlighting relationships. The use of numbering or lettering in the margin, as suggested in 3 above, can help here to identify and clarify such relationships.

7 Establish the causes of the problems

Look for hidden as well as obvious problems. Remember that an obvious problem is often only the symptom of a deeper problem. An identification of such symptoms can often help in the identification of the problem.

- Define the problems.
- Look for relationships between problems.
- Examine whether or not there is any similarity with a real-life situation within your knowledge.
- Analyse the problems and try to determine the causes. Once you have identified a problem it is worth looking to see if that problem has had an effect somewhere else.

Avoid jumping to conclusions before all possibilities have been examined.

When analysing the case you are likely to have to draw some conclusions and use your judgement based on the facts presented to you. You must be careful in doing so to ensure that you do not invent things or draw conclusions which contradict information in the case.

Be careful when making assumptions as these can either be helpful, by focusing the analysis and expediting a solution, or dangerous by diverting or directing your attention along unhelpful lines.

8 Identify and examine possible courses of action or solutions

Evaluate different possible courses of action, examining the validity of each as a solution to the problem(s). If you can identify with a problem and put yourself in the position described in the case, you will often find it easier to decide what course(s) of action you could take to solve the problem.

9 Make decisions and recommendations

These can be short-term or longer-term.

Make sure that, where appropriate, recommendations are specific and detailed and not general and vague.

10 Review the situation

Carry out a review of the situation by re-reading the case study in the light of your findings and recommendations. Modify and amend where necessary.

1.3 Specimen case study
System control

General objectives: To reinforce theoretical learning on system control

To relate theory on system control to a practical situation

To analyse the case and make recommendations

Skills developed: Analysis
Problem-solving
Decision-making

TODD CONSULTANTS

Background

Todd Consultants is a medium-sized organisation based in a county town in a predominantly rural area. The consultancy provides a variety of expertise in IT system implementation and has a wide range of customers with a fairly extensive geographical distribution. The company was established 30 years ago and has always had a good reputation for the quality and reliability of the service which it provides.

Over the past three years the organisation has expanded quite considerably. One reason for this has been the realisation by a growing number of firms of the importance of making effective use of their systems and their staff. Along with the expansion in the organisation's work has come an increase in the permanent staff. This has coincided with a higher than normal rate of staff turnover because of the retiral or resignation of six members of staff.

The management of administration

As with many organisations of a similar size, the work of managing the administration is delegated to one of the Managers, in this case one of the Consultants. As a result of general agreement among the Consultants that something needed to be done to tighten up the control systems, Eileen Frame was given the responsibility of managing the administration and also the specific remit to improve the control systems. Eileen had been with the organisation for five years and had always been rather critical about the control procedures. She started off her new role with great determination and stayed late for a few nights to get things organised.

The new control system

One problem which the organisation had been experiencing was a substantial increase in the cost of stationery and general office supplies. Eileen was certain that there was a lot of waste on the part of the Consultants who, if they did not have the article to hand (eg their pen had "disappeared" or they had left their pencil at home) merely went to the stationery cupboard and took another. Other stationery also disappeared at an alarming rate (eg wallet folders). Eileen determined to keep control of the stationery-cupboard key and to make staff sign for any items they used. To encourage careful use of items she intimated that each month she would circulate a list of who had received what. By doing this she hoped to "shame" some of the staff into taking more care of what they were allocated.

Eileen certainly succeeded in reducing the quantity of stationery and office supplies used each month but, in so doing, irritated some staff and alienated others. One night she inadvertently left the key in the stationery cupboard. When she went to the cupboard in the morning she was sure that quite a number of items were missing and stocks of certain items were definitely depleted! She looked in the supplies record book but no name was recorded as having taken any items since the previous day. When asked, no-one admitted responsibility.

There were quite a few resentful comments made by many of the staff about lack of trust and also about the time they spent filling in forms to get a pen or a roll of sellotape. They were heard to suggest that the time and energy could have been better spent trying to reduce the cost of photocopying which was getting out of hand.

Travel expenses

Another area where there had been mistakes, delays and general problems was in the paying of travel expenses. To improve matters here, Eileen introduced some new forms - five in all. She was very disappointed two months later when she reviewed the system to find a substantial number of staff still submitting completed photocopies of the old forms which did not permit the level of analysis provided by the new forms. Two of the staff to whom she spoke about this said that they did not have time to spend trying to decide which form they should be completing. They complained that it would take a "Philadelphia lawyer" to complete the form and that, in any case, they felt that half of the information was unnecessary.

One of the other controls that Eileen instigated was the placing of a ceiling on the spending in each category. She was again very disappointed to receive a claim for two nights' hotel accommodation from one member of staff who, the records indicated, had always claimed a much smaller amount in the past when she had visited that area because she stayed with a friend. Eileen inquired if the friend was unwell. The member of staff retorted forcibly that her friend was quite well and that she would like to have stayed with her but, under the new system, could not have claimed the cost of taking her friend out for a meal. The new controls only allowed a claim for one person and, according to the member of staff, did not even cover the cost of one person eating in a reasonable restaurant.

Telephone costs

Another area where costs had been rising steeply was that of telephone calls. Comments were made about this and Eileen realised that she had better do something about it. Given the problems with the other controls she had instigated and the general annoyance and frustration among staff, she decided to discuss the control system for telephone costs with the Senior Consultant. They first of all examined the bills over the past three years and established target figures which they thought would require some restraint and control on the part of the Consultants but which were achievable. Eileen then circulated information to staff on the new system and guidelines on how the savings could be achieved. She indicated that she would be analysing the itemised telephone bills and comparing them with the target figures. If there were "problem areas", an investigation would be carried out to ascertain the reason for the deviation and to take appropriate action if necessary.

Everyone seemed reasonably happy with the proposal and, for a time, it was noticeable that staff were being more careful. When the first bill was received the organisation was seen to be meeting its target. Unfortunately, as often happens, because Eileen was very busy for the next few months she did not manage to compare the bills with the targets. It was not until some time later therefore that she realised that one member of staff had been ignoring the guidelines for a number of weeks. By then some other members of staff, seeing what was happening, had reverted to their old ways and the bills were just as high as they had ever been.

ACTION

1. Read the case and identify any problems being experienced by Todd Consultants and, in particular, those which relate to system control.

2. Examine the causes of the various problems.

3. Make recommendations which you think would solve the problems.

4. Identify and examine any instances of good practice in establishing system controls.

GUIDELINE ANSWER TO THE CASE

There now follows a guideline answer to the case. It is important to remember that there may be several acceptable answers to a case. This would certainly be the situation for the answers to Action 3. There is less flexibility in what is acceptable as an answer to Actions 1 and 2 since they are identifying problems and causes, and creativity is not appropriate in such situations. Another point which is worthy of note is that it may not be necessary, nor even desirable, to give separate answers to each Action. What is likely to be much more important is that each Action is dealt with satisfactorily. The linking of at least two Actions may prevent unnecessary repetition and may improve the logical flow of the answer.

Problems and causes

1 Lack of acceptability of a system

One of the main factors which influences the success of any control system is its acceptability to those who are being controlled.

In the case study there is clear evidence that the new system for controlling the issuing of stationery and general supplies is not acceptable to staff since we are told that the staff resent the system because of the time they spend filling in the forms. The reason for the lack of acceptability is not only the time factor but also the general feeling that this is not the most efficient use of time and energy.

There is also some lack of acceptability of the system for travel expense claim forms. The case states that many of the staff felt that they were too difficult to complete and that much of the information requested was, in any case, unnecessary.

2 The control systems not dealing with all the critical areas

To be effective, any organisational control system must deal with all the areas which are critical to the success of the organisation.

There is inference, in the remarks made by staff, that Todd Consultants is not attempting to control the important issue of photocopying costs. The opinion of many staff that this important area is not being controlled has added to their resentment of the system for controlling stationery and office supplies which they see as being of less significance.

3 A control system not always being understandable to those involved

If any system, regardless of what type, is to be successful it must be understood by those involved. If it is not understood, the procedures are unlikely to be followed and this will lead to problems and a potential breakdown of the system.

It is quite obvious from the confusion over which travel form to use and the difficulties being experienced by staff in completing the forms, that there is a widespread lack of understanding of the system.

4 Too much petty control reducing staff morale

If controls are considered to be petty they will be irritating and, where these continue, morale will be affected. This in turn will have implications not only for the likely success of the control system but also for other aspects of organisational life.

In the case study the staff indicated that they regarded the stationery and supplies control system as being petty. They showed this by linking the opinion about the amount of time required to comply with the system with the examples of relatively inexpensive items being controlled. This is reinforced by the staff comments about the system being an inefficient use of time and energy.

Statements which speak of staff annoyance and frustration give a clear pointer to there being problems with morale.

5 Lack of trust results in lack of responsibility

There is normally a direct link between the trust which is placed in the staff and the willingness of the staff to act responsibly. In most cases the realisation that someone is trusting you to do something acts as a control mechanism which encourages responsibility and reduces the need for other more formal controls.

It is clear from the case study that the staff feel that they are not being trusted. Not only is this likely to lead to a *future* reduction in the responsibility that staff are prepared to accept but it would appear that it has already done so. Support for this statement comes from the information given about the non-recording of stationery removed from the cupboard when the key was accidentally left in the lock.

6 The effect of the control system is not consistent with its aim

If a control system is to be effective, its imposition must lead to the achievement of the system's objective. If it does not achieve the objective, the credibility and acceptability of the system will be reduced.

Evidence in the case study of a lack of consistency between the effect of the system and the aim of the system comes in the information about the member of staff claiming the cost of two nights in a hotel. The aim of the controls was to reduce the expenses claimed for travel. Because of the restrictive nature of the system (ie the controls placing ceilings on different categories of spending and only permitting claims for one person) the result was the opposite to what was intended, ie instead of a claim being lower than previously, it was now higher.

Another potential problem may be the level of the meal allowance. It should be noted, however, that the problem may not be that the allowance is too low but rather that the member of staff is expecting too much.

7 Lack of flexibility

Lack of flexibility in a system is likely to cause problems since an exceptional circumstance cannot be accommodated by an exceptional modification to the system. The imposition of the existing system on the exceptional circumstance is often likely to have undesirable implications or effects.

Inability of the system to deal with a claim for a meal for two people shows an inflexibility which has certainly brought undesirable results. The outcome of the imposition of the control is directly opposite to that for which the control was intended.

8 Deviations from the control procedures are not being identified quickly enough

The longer it takes to identify a deviation from the control procedures the greater the likelihood of affecting the outcome of the system's operation.

The delay in Eileen discovering the deviation from the guidelines for reducing telephone costs affected the outcome of the system to such an extent that the aim of the system was not achieved. The reason for the delay was in itself a deviation from the control procedures.

Recommendations for remedying the problems

1 In order to improve acceptability of the control systems it would be advisable to hold discussions with relevant staff (ie representatives of the different groups who will be controlled by the systems). This allows them to make a contribution about any special factors or constraints which would have to be considered.

The discussions would also provide Eileen with an opportunity to explain the rationale behind the systems and the benefits which they will bring. In this way, she should be able to reduce resistance to the systems when they are finally implemented. Since we are told that the Consultants all agreed that the systems needed tightening up, there is unlikely to be resistance to the general idea of control.

Thereafter, Eileen should analyse all the information she has received and modify the systems where necessary to ensure that they maximise efficiency and effectiveness while, at the same time, being acceptable to the staff. The fact that they have had an input to the planning stage (or, in this case, the remedial action) is likely to make them more ready to accept the final systems even if these vary from what they had envisaged. One complication which can arise, however, is that someone may feel he/she has put forward an excellent idea which has subsequently been rejected or ignored. If this is likely to happen, it would be advisable for the designer of the systems to have a further discussion with that individual before the details of the systems are made known:

- to explain why the idea had not been adopted
- to stress, if possible, how valuable the idea had been in helping to formulate the final plan
- to indicate how much the willingness to make a contribution was appreciated
- to indicate considerable regret that it had not been possible to adopt the idea.

By doing this, future resentment and opposition can often be overcome and hopefully the individual will be prepared in future to co-operate again in a similar situation.

2 It is important to examine all aspects of the problem and to assign importance to each aspect. It may well be that a simple control system for one of the less important aspects is introduced first because it can be done simply and quickly. It is vital, however, that the system designer ensures all important aspects are dealt with as quickly as possible and that he/she is not seen to be ignoring one of them. In this case, Eileen needs to review the situation immediately to assess whether any areas requiring a control system have been ignored. If such areas do exist (eg photocopying) they should be tackled as quickly as possible.

3 A good system should be simple to understand as well as being effective. It is important therefore for the system designer to ensure that the system is understandable and as simple as possible. The more complicated a system, the more likely there are to be problems with its operation.

The next stage is to make sure that everyone is aware of what the system is and what the procedures are. It is advisable to document the procedures and to distribute this documentation since everyone may not fully understand a verbal explanation or may subsequently forget some of the details. For some important or more complex systems, verbal and written methods are used to make sure that the system is fully understood.

In this case, Eileen's review process has highlighted the need for her to re-examine the system for controlling travel expenses, to ensure that it is efficient, effective and understandable and that all information being requested is required. She also requires to review any documentation she provided on the operation of the system and amend it as necessary to ensure that it is clear, as simple as possible and has been distributed to everyone concerned.

4 It is important when designing any system to examine the need for that system and compare this with the demands of the system operation. (If the balance is wrong, the system should be revised or removed. In reviewing the design of a system it must always be remembered that the imposition of what are seen as "petty" control systems will most likely bring more adverse results than positive ones.)

In the case, Eileen needs to review the system for issuing stationery and general supplies and to modify it, where appropriate, to ensure that it is not seen to be unnecessarily time-consuming and restrictive. It may be that the answer lies in designing a different control system altogether. The meal allowance in the travel expense system should also be reviewed to ensure that it has been set at a reasonable level.

5 Once again, balance is important. A system which appears to be distrustful of staff will not encourage them to act responsibly and may have the opposite effect. Total trust in some areas, however, is often not the answer since staff may be tempted to take advantage of this.

In the case, Eileen needs to modify the stationery-control system to remove the feeling of distrust that is being given to staff. She will need to remember that it is often more difficult to dispel an idea once it has been formed, than it is to prevent it from forming in the first place.

6 The outcome of a good system will be consistent with its aims. A good system should have an in-built flexibility to cope with exceptional circumstances.

In the case, Eileen needs to review the travel expenses system to provide sufficient flexibility to enable a reasonable claim to be made for entertainment expenses rather than the much more expensive hotel accommodation bill.

7 If a system is to be successful, the procedures must be followed.

Eileen must make sure that she follows her control procedures in order to identify any problem areas at the earliest possible stage.

Good practices identified

Most of the good practices identified relate to the system for controlling telephone costs and are as follows:

1 There was planning before the system was implemented which included discussions with relevant staff. (It is difficult to tell in this instance, without further information, whether or not the process might have been improved by including some other staff in the discussions.)

2 The system included the establishment of acceptable standards (ie the target cost figures for each period) which were notified to those to whom the control system applied.

3 The system was designed to measure the actual performance.

4 The system then compared the actual performance with the target figures.

5 The system allowed for investigation of any unacceptable deviation, and amendment where appropriate.

The other good practice identified was the review/monitoring of the operation of the new system. This occurred with the system for travel expenses and enabled identification of significant problems in the system which would require further investigation. A good system will also allow for periodic reviews of the effectiveness and efficiency of the operation of the system, as well as an examination of the system's necessity and validity (eg to make sure that all information requested is necessary and sufficient).

SECTION 2
ORGANISATIONAL STRUCTURE AND PRINCIPLES

An understanding of organisational structure and principles is a vital component of the study of administrative management. Someone who does not have such an understanding is unlikely to make a success of managing administration since the administrative systems must operate within the structure of the organisation and follow general principles of organisation. For this reason, organisational structure and principles is the first area to be examined in this book. The section examines three important areas: centralisation/decentralisation, organisational relationships and delegation.

The decision on whether to have centralised or decentralised (often referred to as "distributed") systems is particularly relevant at the present time. A number of years ago there was a general move to centralise systems in order to improve effectiveness and control and to gain the benefits of economy of scale. With the major developments in personal computers, networking and telecommunications, however, there has been a change in many organisations in recent years in favour of a more distributed system for computing while still retaining the benefits of centralised policy-making and user support. Since computerisation affects many of the systems where centralisation/decentralisation is an issue, it will be necessary for all organisations in the future to re-examine their systems to ensure that their preferred option for each system is the most efficient one for the organisation.

Good relationships between departments and staff within an organisation are vital if the organisation is to function as an entity. Many of the problems which occur in organisations, however, do so because staff do not understand or do not follow the correct channels of communication. Such problems not only affect the operation of a system but can also have major implications for interpersonal relationships between individuals in a department and in different departments. This in turn is likely to affect the level of efficiency of the organisation as a whole.

One of the principles of organisation with which there are often problems is delegation. The success of any organisation consisting of more that one person is dependent on efficient delegation. It is therefore vital that staff know what can and should be delegated, what cannot and should not be delegated, and how to delegate effectively.

Case 2.1
Centralisation/decentralisation

General objectives: To reinforce learning on organisational relationships and the issue of centralisation/decentralisation

To relate theories on centralisation/decentralisation to a practical situation

To analyse the case and write a report on the findings

Skills developed: Analysis
Problem-solving
Decision-making
Report-writing
Communication

GIBSON FINANCIAL SERVICES

Background

Gibson Financial Services is an expanding organisation which provides a large range of financial services to many different types of business. The organisation is situated in a city centre and, because of fairly rapid expansion, made the decision five years ago to take a lease on offices in another building. As a result, the organisation now has offices in buildings on both sides of a busy main road. For most departments this had caused few problems since, to a large extent, they were fairly self-contained. Departments such as Personnel which have responsibility across all departments, are situated in the original building, which is the larger.

Problems with records management

Problems related to the maintenance of records, however, have been occurring over the last few years. At present each department is responsible for storing and managing its own records, including indenting for its own records storage equipment. As a result, there are several different records management systems and equipment in use throughout the organisation.

18 Administrative Management Case Studies

One issue which has caused significant problems is that a customer dealing with more than one department could well have files in each department. The organisation has received complaints from one or two customers who felt that they were being treated as "new" by one department when in fact they had been very closely involved with the organisation for many years. Attempts to avoid this type of situation had not been totally successful. Some time was also spent in copying customers' documents which related to more than one department. On a few occasions a copy had not been sent to another department, which caused subsequent problems and irritation to the customer.

Another problem which arose in three cases was that one department opened a file for a "new customer" without realising that, for some time, the same customer had been causing major problems to another department. Had staff in the new department known of the problems, they would have dealt with the situation very differently.

Staffing issues

The distributed nature of the records management had caused other problems. Some departments had got very far behind with their records management and had large piles of documents waiting to be filed. Two of these departments had requested the employment of some temporary staff to help clear the backlog. When a member of staff from the Personnel Department contacted the relevant departments, it became clear that the cause of the backlog was not the same in both cases.

In the first case, the department had had a particularly busy spell with a significant increase in business, which had coincided with their being short-staffed for a few weeks because of illness. The Personnel Department arranged for a temporary transfer of a junior member of staff from another department which was less busy. Despite working hard, the staff member's achievement in the first week was disappointing. The reason for this was that he had had to spend so much time learning the records management system which was quite different from that in his own department.

The problem in the second department was more related to inefficiency on the part of staff not following proper records management procedures because they disliked that aspect of the work. As a result, a lot of time was being wasted because staff could not quickly find documents and sometimes did not even realise that they existed. This latter situation had led to letters of complaint from customers. There were also problems in that department with documents being misfiled through carelessness and lack of understanding on the part of two of the departmental staff.

Equipment requests

Concern was expressed by the Purchasing Officer about the significant rise in the departmental requests for additional records management equipment - in many cases filing cabinets. He was certain that, while departments probably required additional space for records, many of the cabinets, if purchased, would not be completely filled.

ACTION

1 Read the case study and identify the problems facing Gibson Financial Services.

2 Examine what benefits you think a centralised records management system could bring to the organisation.

3 Do you think a centralised records management system would have any drawbacks for the organisation? If so, identify and examine the drawbacks.

4 You have been called in to investigate the problems facing Gibson Financial Services and to make recommendations for solving these problems. Write a report detailing and justifying your recommendations.

Case 2.2
Organisational relationships

General objectives: To identify the different types of organisational relationships

To gain an understanding of problems which can arise when the organisational relationship structure breaks down

To analyse the case and recommend a solution to the current difficulties

Skills developed: Analysis
Constructing an organisational chart
Problem-solving
Decision-making
Report-writing
Communication

FLEMING ENTERPRISES PLC

Background

Fleming Enterprises plc is a large company with various sections of administrative work (eg reception and mail; telephones; reprographics; records management; document production) under the control of the Administrative Manager.

Personnel involved in the case

Albert Swan	Managing Director
Karen Grant	Personnel Officer
John Jack	Data Processing Manager
James Collins	Administrative Manager
Arlene Darroch	Reception and Mail Supervisor
Walter Ross	Reprographics Supervisor
Rhona Dale	Document Production Supervisor
Jennifer Morrison	Telephone Supervisor
Robert Walker	Records Supervisor
Jane Black	Personal Assistant

Events of last few months

Over the last few months James has become very concerned that his control of the department is being eroded. One or two of the Supervisors, particularly Arlene Darroch, Reception and Mail Supervisor, and Walter Ross, Reprographics Supervisor, have not been informing him of some of their actions, which have subsequently been called into question by his superior. To counteract this, he has issued instructions that ALL contact with other departments must be made through him and that a Supervisor must gain his prior approval before coming to any arrangements with other Supervisors. Morale in the office has decreased noticeably since this announcement.

Events of the last two weeks

During the last two weeks the following events have occurred:

1 James Collins had an angry exchange of words with his superior, Albert Swan, the Managing Director. On his way to lunch one day, Mr Swan had stopped to have a friendly chat with Rhona Dale, the Document Production Supervisor. During the conversation, he asked her how she was getting on and whether or not she was experiencing any major problems with the new word processing equipment. James took exception to Mr Swan asking this latter question of Rhona and said that he felt Mr Swan should have spoken to him directly about it.

2 James Collins had an argument with Karen Grant, the Personnel Officer. Without consulting him, Karen had held a telephone conversation with Jennifer Morrison, Telephone Supervisor, over the company procedures for early retirement.

3 Robert Walker, Records Supervisor, announced his unwillingness to continue as the departmental nominee on a working party. This working party, chaired by John Jack, the Data Processing Manager, is examining the possibility of computerising all records. Robert stated that he could no longer make any valuable contribution as every suggestion he made had to be approved by James Collins.

4 James Collins announced that, while he was on holiday for a week, Supervisors should report to Jane Black, his Personal Assistant for the last 12 years, who would handle everything.

ACTION

1 Identify the problems which appear in the above case study and, in particular, those relating to formal and informal organisational relationships.

2 Examine each problem and its causes.

3 Construct an appropriate section of Fleming's organisational chart showing, as far as possible, the various relationships outlined in the case.

4 Assume that you are a communications expert who has been called into Fleming Enterprises plc to examine the problems relating to organisational relationships and to write a *formal report* including recommendations for solving the problems.

   Present the section of the report which deals with *informal organisational relationships*.

Case 2.3
Delegation

General objectives: To reinforce learning on principles of delegation

To relate theories of delegation to a practical situation

To analyse the case and draw conclusions

To prepare a set of guidelines on delegation

Skills developed: Analysis
Problem-solving
Decision-making
Communication

ABBEY STORES

Background

Abbey Stores is a fairly large department store in a busy market town. It was established in 1922 and, over the years, has built up an enviable reputation for quality and reliability. It has always been in the control of different members of one family, who have adopted a caring attitude to staff and to the local community. Salaries, although not high, have always equated to those paid by similar organisations. Morale on the whole has always been good and the staff have taken a pride in working for the company.

Ladies Fashion Department

The Ladies Fashion Department is one of the largest Departments in the store with a number of sub-sections within it. The current Manager, Margot Lawson, was appointed to the job nine months ago, having worked for Abbey Stores in a number of Departments for 22 years. Since becoming Manager she has been the instigator of a number of changes - one of which resulted from her attendance at a management training course prior to her current appointment. An aspect which was stressed during the course was the importance of delegation. Margot felt that delegation of some of her responsibilities, as well as being good for staff development, might prevent her from having a stroke like her predecessor, who had always appeared harassed despite working very long hours both in the store and at home. With some difficulty she managed to persuade the management to agree to make a very small addition to the salary of those to whom she planned to delegate a reasonable amount of responsibility.

At her first Departmental meeting she outlined her policy for the Department over the next few months. At the same time she stated that she intended to delegate quite a number of duties to different members of staff since she knew from personal experience how capable they were. There was some surprise among the staff about her plans. Vera Smith, a young woman in her late 20s who had been with Abbey Stores for five years and who was enthusiastic and ambitious, nodded approvingly. On the other hand, Betty Carr, who was in her 50s, muttered something about people getting a job and passing all the real work to other folk. She had worked in the Ladies Fashion Department for 26 years and had been very disappointed at yet again being passed over for the management job. She felt that her experience and loyal support of the last two Managers should have counted for more than it obviously had done.

Delegation

Shortly after the Departmental meeting Margot asked Vera Smith to come and see her. She indicated to Vera that she had noticed how enthusiastic and hard working she was and what good ideas she had. Margot continued by saying that she would like Vera to take over the development of the new boutique section for the younger woman, which was a vital part of the company's new sales drive to update its image. She indicated that, since Vera was in that age group herself, she would be given quite a free hand to choose what styles to order.

Margot realised that she had better also see Betty Carr. She was aware of Betty's disappointment and was anxious to make some overtures to dispel the "frostiness" which had arisen between them. She approached Betty about looking after the coat and jacket section which had been going through a slightly difficult time recently with the move away from coats and jackets to anoraks and other casual garments. Margot felt that this was a Department which would present Betty with the type of challenge to give her a new focus for her career. She also recognised that Betty was rather traditional in her taste in clothes and that she would be better in a section like coats and jackets than in dresses or separates where fashion played a more important part. Betty indicated that she did not know whether or not she wanted to run the section, given that she had not been considered good enough for a management role. Margot chose to ignore these comments but decided that Betty should not have direct contact with the representatives, as she was a little concerned about her ability to deal with some of them. Instead, she told Betty to pass all the orders through her. Margot knew that she would be seeing the representatives anyway about the separates and dresses and could deal with Betty's orders at the same time.

Problems in the coat and jacket section

When Margot received Betty's orders she examined them very carefully and made quite a few changes. Unfortunately, because she was very busy, she did not normally have time to discuss the changes with Betty before handing the orders over to the representatives. This caused a major confusion the first time a changed order was delivered, as Betty treated the change as a mistake and contacted the supplier accordingly. It took quite a few days to sort out the problem and, in the meantime, relations between Betty and the suppliers became rather strained. When Betty found out what had happened she was furious and complained loudly about not being trusted and not being allowed to get on with the job. She also complained bitterly about a discussion Margot had had with the other Assistant in the coat and jacket section where Margot had asked him to change a display which she thought would be more attractive if displayed in another way.

Six months later

About six months after her discussions with Vera and Betty, Margot was called in by the Senior Manager of the store. He stated that he was very concerned that the recent figures for her Department indicated a fall in both turnover and profits. He indicated his particular concern about the boutique section which had been vital to the success of the firm's new marketing drive and which had proved to be a bit of a disaster. Not only had it made a substantial loss but he had received a number of letters from regular and valued customers stating that the clothes in that section were very poor quality and of such "way out" designs that no-one who was likely to shop in Abbey Stores would be remotely interested in them.

Margot bit her lip and said that it was all the fault of Vera Smith in whom she had had great confidence. She stated that Vera had not had any discussions with her about plans for the boutique but that she, Margot, had not wanted to interfere. She promised to have a discussion with Vera and to move her to another section.

When Margot broached the matter later with Vera, she had been angry and stated that she had done exactly what Margot had asked her to do. She asked how she was to know that the management wanted something much less adventurous and, in her opinion, rather staid. She added that if this was the management's attitude she did not think she wanted to work in Abbey Stores any longer. Her parting shot was that she did not think very highly of a management who paid her a mere pittance for all the extra work and responsibility and yet were only too happy to make a scapegoat of her when things went wrong.

ACTION

1 Examine the case study and identify any evidence of good or bad practice in delegation.

2 Of what theories of delegation are these examples of good or bad practice?

3 Do you identify any other problems highlighted by the case? If so, what are they and what are the causes of the problems?

4 The case suggests that Margot's predecessor very seldom delegated anything. Give reasons why some Managers seem reluctant to delegate tasks to appropriate members of staff?

5 Prepare a set of guidelines on how to delegate effectively.

SECTION 3
EFFECTIVE COMMUNICATION

Effective communication is vital to the success of any organisation. While all organisations would agree with the truth of this statement, most would also agree that communication is one of the most problematic areas for any organisation. It is certainly an issue about which employees frequently complain. Communication problems, however, are not restricted to the internal organisational environment. Problems occur in communication with customers and suppliers and in some instances lead to a loss of future orders.

Because communication is central to all areas of organisational life, issues and problems of communication are featured in all of the sections and most of the case studies in this book. It is, however, important that some more concentrated attention is given to certain aspects of communication. This section will therefore look at three aspects.

Attention will first be given to the barriers to communication and how these can be overcome, since these are often the reason why communication is not effective. The remainder of the section will examine two areas which cause particular problems for organisations - report-writing and telephone techniques. The topic of meetings and minute-writing, which is another area of considerable concern to organisations, will be dealt with in Section 6 under "meetings".

Case 3.1
Barriers to communication

General objectives: To reinforce understanding of factors which prevent effective communication

To relate theory of communication to a practical situation

To analyse the case and make recommendations

Skills developed: Analysis
Problem-solving
Decision-making

GEORGE & TURNER PLC

Background

Andrew Gray is the Marketing Manager of a large, long-established organisation. Within his Department he has an Assistant Manager, three Heads of Section and 14 Administrators/Clerks. Over the last few years there has been quite a significant turnover of staff due to resignations, two retirals and one promotion to Head of Section in another department.

Up until about 20 years ago, the organisation had the reputation of being fairly traditional and very reliable, if somewhat dull. Since then things have gradually begun to change - partly because of a campaign to reverse a trend towards a decline in market share and partly because of a change in the senior management team. One noticeable fact has been the campaign to change the corporate image from one where the main aims are accuracy and reliability to one which places much more emphasis on speedy response to customer enquiries and a high rate of turnover through offering a much wider selection of products at lower average prices. The changes brought some initial improvement but not the longed-for significant increase in profits. In the last few years the organisation has once again had a struggle to retain its market share.

Problems in the Marketing Department

As one would expect, the organisational problems and how to resolve them have been on the agenda of almost every Management meeting over the last few months. At one of the fairly recent Management meetings, the Customer Services Manager had submitted a paper which highlighted a significant increase in the number of complaints from customers about lack of efficiency in a whole range of areas. There was general agreement that an improvement in organisational efficiency was vital and had to be brought about speedily. The management responded, first of all, by issuing a notice reminding all staff of the need to tighten up procedures and, in particular, any procedures which directly affected customers or the public at large.

A more detailed investigation indicated that one of the Departments which had most often featured in customer complaints was the Marketing Department. Although the complaints themselves differed, there was a common theme to many of them - communication.

Customer complaints

A complaint voiced by three customers was that staff in the Marketing Department had, on several occasions, given a verbal quotation over the telephone which was different from the information in the written quotation which followed. Two of the customers indicated that, had they not read the written quotation closely, they might not have spotted the difference since the wording was rather lengthy and unclear. The customers did point out that their requests were not standard requests but that, regardless of that, they had not expected to be given incorrect information.

A second area about which there had been several complaints from customers of many years' standing was the very impersonal and formal responses which they were now getting to telephone or written enquiries. They expressed much regret that the emphasis on personal attention and knowledge of customers, which had always been a hallmark of George & Turner, seemed to have disappeared.

A number of irate letters had also come from some old and valued customers about a piece of correspondence they had recently received from the Marketing Department. The offending document had been circulated with the latest catalogue and very forcibly suggested that customers should pay more attention when writing orders. It said that mistakes and omissions were likely to cause delays and, in the longer term, higher prices, as George & Turner would have to pass on to customers the cost of correcting the errors.

Departmental communication problems

Problems with communication were not restricted to external communication. Discussions with Departmental staff indicated that they were also unhappy about communication. A number of problems were highlighted.

The first of these was the complaint that Departmental staff had several times been blamed by staff in another Department for something which was not their fault. The problem, according to them, lay in the fact that Andrew Gray had not passed a vital piece of information to them. They were even more annoyed when Andrew had disclaimed any responsibility for the confusion which had arisen and had indicated that they had been given written notes of guidance on the matter. He had said that they should not have relied solely on the verbal explanation which he had given to them when they had expressed difficulty in following the rather technical information contained in the guidelines.

Another member of the Departmental staff had been very disgruntled recently. A year ago she had made a suggestion about a marketing technique which she had felt would significantly improve the Department's turnover. At the time Andrew Gray had dismissed the idea and refused to spend more than two minutes listening to the details as he said that it would not prove attractive to customers in the prevailing economic climate. Now, one year on, he had put an almost identical proposal to a recent Management meeting. They had unanimously approved the proposal and in the next issue of the organisational journal had congratulated him on thinking of the idea, which they expected to be highly successful because of a recent Government announcement.

The Assistant Manager had complained bitterly to Andrew about the lack of co-operation he had been experiencing from Andrea, one of the Section Heads. He said that, in the past, he had always found her to be very willing and enthusiastic. When he was asked by Andrew if he could remember what had triggered the change, he said that he was not sure. The only time he had said anything negative to Andrea was about a month ago when he had had to speak sharply to her about time-keeping after he had passed her and two other section staff lingering in the canteen looking at holiday photographs.

Complaints from other departments

Several staff from other Departments had also complained about the Marketing Department. The Chairman of one of the sub-committees had stated that they had not been able to make a decision in time to benefit from special terms because Andrew had not produced a paper he had been asked to prepare for a particular Management meeting. The Meetings Clerk had delayed sending out the papers for the meeting until the very last minute, hoping to get Andrew's paper. Although Andrew brought the paper to the meeting, they had not been able to discuss the matter since no-one had had time to read and digest the paper.

Another Manager had been heard to speak angrily about Andrew not doing something important and denying all knowledge of being asked to undertake the job. This Manager insisted that he had spoken to Andrew about it, as he distinctly remembered having had difficulty in finding him and eventually catching him just before he dashed out of the door to go and visit an important customer. He clearly remembered Andrew saying that he had no time to deal with it then as he was already late for his appointment but assuring him that the matter would be attended to as soon as he returned from the visit.

ACTION

1 Read the case study and identify any problems which are currently being experienced by George & Turner plc and, in particular, those relating to communication.

2 Examine the causes of the problems and recommend a course of action which George & Turner should follow to eliminate these problems.

Case 3.2
Report-writing

General objectives: To reinforce learning on the principles of report-writing

To gain an understanding of some of the problems which can result from poor report-writing

To develop skill in report-writing

To draft a set of guidelines

Skills developed: Analysis
Problem-solving
Decision-making
Report-writing
Documenting procedures
Communication

CLARK ENERGY CONSERVATION LTD

Background

Clark Energy Conservation Ltd is an organisation which provides a range of services related to energy conservation for companies of varying sizes in a wide geographical distribution. The company was established in the 1970s at the time when double-glazing was becoming popular as a means of reducing fuel costs. The years since then have seen significant changes in the company, resulting from the growing national concern about energy conservation. One major change has been the company's diversification into a number of other areas - all related to energy conservation. Another factor which brought great change has been the huge growth in the company in the last 10 years thanks to the enterprise and vigorous marketing of the current management team. During that time two branches have been established to meet the needs in their surrounding areas.

Administrative problems

A substantial and speedy increase in size, which includes the hiring of many new staff, often brings with it a number of problems and this was certainly the case with Clark Energy Conservation. When the organisation was fairly small there was not the same need for a formalisation of administrative procedures and, as with many similar organisations, what procedures there were developed in a fairly *ad hoc* way. Part of the reason for this was that most of the original staff lacked any formal training in administration. It was, however, recognised that the situation had to change, and over the years more formal procedures were developed in many areas.

Reports

One area where there was much greater activity and which was occupying a lot of time for many staff was report-writing. The requirement to produce more reports had come with the increase in turnover and number of staff. Only in this way could management keep abreast of the work which was being undertaken and of the jobs for which tenders were being submitted. Reports were also required on a wide range of other topics.

Considerable concern had been expressed by some of the management team over the quality of many of the reports and the fact that, in a number of cases, staff who required to have the information in a report were not sent a copy. One of the Managers, David Lang, had complained bitterly about the time he had wasted in trying to find out who had written a report which he found lying on the Managing Director's desk. He had been waiting while the Managing Director dealt with an urgent phone call when his eye caught a sentence in the report which suggested that the subject matter was one of considerable interest to himself.

When the Managing Director came off the phone, David asked him about the report. The Managing Director indicated that he was not too sure of the subject of the report as he had not had time to read it. He added that he was also not quite certain why it had been sent to him and that he did not know from whom it had originated. He made some suggestions, however, of Departments and members of staff whom David could try.

When David did eventually track down the authors of the report, he discovered that the report had in fact been written some four months earlier. He also discovered that the report concerned a problem which had been dealt with three months ago and did not refer to the problem about which David was concerned.

Report on stationery costs

One matter which was causing considerable alarm in the organisation was the rising cost of stationery. An examination of the breakdown of expenses indicated that much of this was attributable to the quantity of paper being used. Although increases in the cost of paper had certainly been a factor, the substantial rise in the amount of paper being used was the more significant factor.

The topic was discussed at a Management meeting and Janice Norman, the Manager in charge of general administration, undertook to carry out an investigation and submit a formal report containing recommendations on the issue to a subsequent Management meeting. Janice asked Ronald, her recently-appointed Assistant, to carry out the investigation, to draft the report and to submit the draft to her for onward transmission as soon as possible.

The report on paper usage

The following is the report Ronald submitted to Janice.

REPORT

Following the instructions given to me I have carried out an investigation and the following is what I found.

The first thing I investigated was the use of the photocopier since this was also a cause of concern as regards cost. One thing I found was that quite a number of staff are taking more copies than they need just in case they run out. They said to me that it cost less for them to take a few extra copies at the time when they were doing the copying than the cost of their having to leave what they were doing and go and take an extra copy at a later point. Although the extra copies do cost money, it seems to me that it might well be more costly for the company to have to pay for them to take single copies later, particularly when, from what they say, they quite often need more copies than the original estimate.

A more serious problem appears to be the amount of paper that has been wasted due to faults in the large photocopier. Over the past few months this photocopier has had a recurring fault which is that a section of the page is so faint that you cannot read it. Unfortunately the fault does not happen all the time and often, because the first copy is good, it is not spotted that later copies are faulty until the whole run has been completed. When this occurs the job has to be redone and this leads to a substantial waste of paper if the run is a long one. The engineers have been out repairing the copier repeatedly and each time they say they have sorted it. Everything works well for a few days and then the fault seems to recur. It certainly seems that we should either be forcing the supplier to give the machine a major overhaul to find the fault or buying a new photocopier.

Waste is also a problem with the WP. I watched a number of staff take several draft printouts of documents for proofreading purposes because they had not checked the screen and run their spell-checker first. They often required a second or third draft because they were a bit careless in proofreading and amending the first draft. I certainly saw a lot of spoiled printouts in the waste bins.

During discussions, the girls indicated that Managers were just as bad. They seem to think that, because you do not have to retype a document, it doesn't really matter if they send it back for editing a few times. I think that there are really four Managers who cause this type of waste. I spoke to two of them. During our discussions they gave me to understand that they were not unhappy with the current situation on document production. They said that they were more unhappy about the waste of paper which had resulted from the management decision to change Form E25. Just before this decision was made they had got their monthly supply printed. All that paper is now being used for scrap because the management wanted the change made right away. There is a rumour going around just now that the same sort of thing is going to happen with forms B57 and B58. Staff think that it might not be imprudent to merge the two documents and could be a good thing in the long run and save quite a lot of paper since a lot of the information on both forms is duplicated and one form could be used to input the information into the computer which could then automatically be transferred to the appropriate files.

While I was speaking to David Lang about this my eye caught a pile of photocopies of papers to be sent out to all the Departments. I picked one up and was slightly horrified to see that it had about 10 pages all single-sided only. When I questioned David as to why they had not used the double-sided facility, he said that he was not too sure but they probably just did not think.

During my investigations I noticed quite a lot of good quality paper (and sometimes headed paper) being used as scrap paper for odd notes, telephone messages or sometimes even just doodles. A not insignificant problem is the amount of paper used for non-business purposes. Although I did not actually see anyone doing this I heard on the grapevine that one or two staff have been known to run off numerous copies of documents (and not always short ones) to be circulated to the members of their sports clubs or other similar clubs. I certainly think that it should be made clear that such activities are not to be countenanced. It may be, of course, that management would consider allowing staff to use the facilities for such purposes provided they did it in their own time and paid an appropriate amount for it.

My last comment is that staff should be encouraged to be careful how they store their stationery. I saw, on a number of occasions, paper being discarded where a corner had been accidentally folded over or where the paper had got dirty and in some instances marked with a coffee stain!

I consider that if the recommendations outlined above are followed there could be a considerable saving in the stationery bill.

ACTION

1   Read the case and comment on the report which Ronald produced for Janice.

2   In your opinion how could it have been improved?

3   What other problems does Clark Energy Conservation seem to have with report-writing? How could they be remedied?

4   Using the information given in the case, redraft the report on paper usage.

5   Draw up a set of guidelines on report-writing which could be given to all relevant staff in Clark Energy Conservation.

Case 3.3
Telephone techniques

General objectives: To gain an understanding of some of the problems involved in telephone techniques

To analyse the case and recommend a solution to the current difficulties

To document a set of procedures

Skills developed: Analysis
Problem-solving
Decision-making
Documenting procedures
Communication

BROWNLEE & SMITH (1)

Background

Brownlee & Smith is a fairly large legal practice with a number of Partners specialising in different legal areas. The practice employs five Senior Secretaries as well as 10 general secretarial and clerical staff who are under the control of the Office Manager, Freda Watkins.

Until recently, Karen Graham has been the Receptionist/Telephonist for the practice. Last month she was promoted to the post of Records Assistant in charge of the new computerised records system and directly responsible to Freda Watkins. Alison Jackson, a sixteen-year-old school-leaver, was appointed as the new Receptionist/Telephonist and had started work three weeks ago. Since Alison was an intelligent girl and had a reference from school which indicated that she "got on well with people", it was expected that she would cope well with the job.

Organisational personnel in the case

Senior Partner   Roger Brownlee
Partners   Lena Smart and James Peters
Senior Secretary   Marjory McLean

Office Manager	Freda Watkins
Records Assistant	Karen Graham
Receptionist/Telephonist	Alison Jackson

Week one

1 Problems occurred from the start. Freda Watkins had to interview Alison at the end of her first week and point out that there had been a number of complaints from various members of staff. Some of the complaints were about the telephone messages written by Alison. A number of the messages had been very long and confusing and the recipients had had to come back to Alison for clarification (which she had often been unable to provide).

On another occasion one of the Partners had been angry when he had been unable to find the telephone number of a prospective client, who had left a message asking the Partner to ring him as soon as possible. When the Partner had consulted Alison she assured him that the caller had not left a telephone number. There were two complaints from incoming callers that they had been left with the extension ringing until they had hung up.

2 Another complaint came from one of the Partners, Lena Smart, who had been antagonised because Alison had told her that there was a telephone call for her and had then been unable to give her any information other than that it was a "lady". Lena had refused to speak to the caller until she knew who it was and what she wanted. Alison had said to the caller that Ms Smart would like to know her name and what she wished to discuss. Alison had then duly reported back to Lena and had told her that it was Barbara Crawford from the *Daily Gazette* who wished to discuss with her the recent report that the practice had made a major blunder in negotiating the purchase of new premises for the local children's home. Lena had been furious as she had realised that she now had no alternative but to speak to Barbara Crawford who was the gossip columnist of the newspaper. An investigation of the procedures involved in the purchase was currently being undertaken by two of the Partners and the issue was scheduled to be discussed by the Partners at a special meeting later that week. Lena sent an angry memo to Freda asking her to speak to Alison about her telephone technique.

3 Roger Brownlee, the Senior Partner, also complained about Alison putting through directly to him a call from a drunk and irate mother who had insisted on speaking to him about the recent court decision to take her two young children into care.

He had been further annoyed by the fact that his meeting with Sir Gavin Mackenzie, an important client, had been interrupted by Alison telephoning to find out if his visitor was a Mr Wallace Smith. Mr Smith's wife had been urgently trying to contact him and had only known that he planned to visit someone in the organisation. (Marjory McLean, Roger's secretary, had been in her office at the time.)

Week two

1. The week after Freda's discussion with Alison, Alison irritated Daniel Spensor, the Managing Director of one of the largest client firms, by answering the telephone with the words "Hello, can I help you?". He asked to speak to James Peters, one of the Partners. Alison had been told by James Peters to say that he was out as he wanted some peace to get on with an urgent report which had been delayed because of constant interruptions that morning. Bearing in mind her interview with Freda Watkins the week before, Alison asked if she could take a message. When she realised who the caller was she became flustered and said "Oh, Mr Spensor! Ah, I think Mr Peters will speak to you. Hang on and I'll ask him." Daniel Spensor was horrified and complained bitterly to James Peters about the quality of staff now being employed.

2. Lena Smart again contacted Freda about Alison. This time she had received a complaint from a potential client. The caller had wasted a significant amount of time trying to contact Lena. The first time he had telephoned, he had been cut off by Alison. When he rang back and asked to speak to Lena, Alison had left him "hanging on" for a considerable time while she tried to find Lena as there was no reply to her extension. He was just about to give up and ring off, when she had come back and reported that she could not find Lena and that one of Lena's colleagues had said that she had met her going out of the side door on her way to an appointment 20 miles away.

   The caller had asked Alison to give Lena a message to telephone him as soon as possible. Alison had been unable to find any telephone message slips and had written the message on a piece of scrap paper intending to transfer it to the correct slip when she found one. As events transpired, she forgot to do so because she became involved with a problem at reception.

3. Alison was trying to deal with the problem at reception when the telephone rang again. She answered it rather brusquely and was immediately reprimanded by Karen Graham who was on the other end of the line and from whom she had received a reprimand earlier in the week for not answering the telephone speedily.

4. Alison was just about to get the number for Karen when once again the telephone rang. This time it was James Peters who had just come in and wanted Alison urgently to look up the telephone directory for the telephone number of a society with whom the organisation had regular dealings. Since Alison realised that this would take her a little time, she decided that she had better get Karen's number first. It took her longer than she had expected to make contact with the person to whom Karen wanted to speak, since the extension was engaged and Alison had to "hold on" for a long while. She was just putting Karen through when the switchboard flashed again. It was James Peters ringing back to find out what on earth was keeping Alison from getting the urgent number for him! He was annoyed with the tone which Alison used in answering this second call and told her so!

ACTION

1 Identify the problems in the case which are related to telephone technique.

2 Analyse the problems, suggesting ways in which they could be overcome.

3 Assume the role of Freda Watkins and draw up a set of procedures on telephone technique which in future could be passed to any new Receptionist/Telephonist.

SECTION 4
GENERAL ADMINISTRATIVE PROCEDURES AND PUBLIC RELATIONS

The efficient functioning of administration is dependent on a number of factors, one of the most important of which is the establishment of good procedures. This is an aspect which in some organisations is unfortunately given a much lower profile than it deserves. One of the reasons for this is that it can be fairly time-consuming and rather boring. It also requires attention to detail which some people find irritating. A further reason why this is often a neglected area is that some people consider it to be rather an unnecessary task since it would be common sense to follow the procedure anyway without sitting down and specially designing it. While this may well be true in some instances, people do not always act logically and very often take short cuts which, if they thought about them properly, they would avoid, realising the potential problems that could result.

Establishing procedures is one thing; documenting them and following them can be quite another. The documenting of procedures can be even more time-consuming and boring, and require great attention to detail. An efficient Department, however, should have its procedures documented so that anyone coming into the Department who is unfamiliar with the procedures can very quickly see what they are and follow them. This can save a Department quite a considerable amount of time and trouble and is particularly important for today's organisation where so many systems are computerised.

Most people slip up in following established procedures at one time or another. The reasons are often related to carelessness. Shortage of time is an excuse which is frequently given for not following some procedure. The irony of such a statement is that more time is usually spent solving a problem which has arisen from not following a procedure than would have been required to follow the procedure in the first place.

This section examines a number of areas, giving particular attention to the correct procedures which should be adopted in each case for the smooth operation of the function or task. The areas which are examined in some detail are: reception; the management of diaries and appointments; the management of travel; and the management of time.

Each one of these areas is vital to the successful administration of an organisation. In themselves they may appear fairly trivial but, if they do not function smoothly, the repercussions can be far from trivial.

Another aspect which is examined is public relations. Each of the areas in the section has a public relations dimension, which has always been an important area for an organisation. In recent years, however, its importance has been more widely recognised and public relations generally now has a much higher profile than was the case previously.

A final aspect which is examined in this section is the subject of working relationships. Along with the major concern among many organisations about organisational culture has come a change in how we view our relationships with colleagues. One view of working relationships which is commonly found today is the idea of people working in teams where each team member has a specific and valuable contribution to make to the functioning of the team as a whole. This approach has coincided with the move away from the idea of an employee/boss relationship and has continued to develop as the work of organisations grows more complex and it becomes less and less feasible for any one individual to have a detailed knowledge of the whole.

Case 4.1
Reception

General objectives: To gain an understanding of some of the problems involved in reception techniques

To analyse the case and discuss the causes of the problems

To present the analysis of the problems and future recommendations in the form of a report

Skills developed: Analysis
Problem-solving
Decision-making
Report-writing
Communication

BROWNLEE & SMITH (2)

Background

Brownlee & Smith is a fairly large legal practice with a number of Partners specialising in different legal areas. The practice employs five Senior Secretaries as well as 10 general secretarial and clerical staff who are under the control of the Office Manager, Freda Watkins.

Until recently, Karen Graham has been the Receptionist/Telephonist for the practice. Last month she was promoted to the post of Records Assistant in charge of the new computerised records system and directly responsible to Freda Watkins. Alison Jackson, a sixteen-year-old school-leaver, was appointed as the new Receptionist/Telephonist and started work three weeks ago. Since Alison was an intelligent girl and had a reference from school which indicated that she "got on well with people", it was expected that she would cope well with the job.

Organisational personnel in the case

Senior Partner	Roger Brownlee
Partners	George Smart and James Peters
Senior Secretary	Marjory McLean

Office Manager   Freda Watkins
Records Assistant   Karen Graham
Receptionist/Telephonist   Alison Jackson

Week one

For the first two days things went well for Alison, who was very anxious to be helpful and efficient. On the third day, however, things began to go wrong. It started with a new client calling to see one of the Partners whose office was some distance from the entrance. Alison started to give the client directions but found it difficult and decided that it would be quicker to take him there herself. She realised that it would leave the reception desk unattended for a short time but considered it was important that the new client was not left to wander about the organisation. She felt it was unlikely that anyone would call during the few minutes of her absence and even if anyone did, he/she would not have long to wait.

What Alison did not expect was that the Partner would be out of his room and that she would have to spend some time looking for him. On her way back she met George Smart who stopped to ask her how she was settling in. By the time she answered his questions and returned to her desk, she found two people waiting, neither of whom was at all pleased at her delay. One was the driver of a delivery van who was waiting to get Alison's signature on a delivery note for several heavy packages of stationery. In order to minimise the carrying distance he had parked right outside the office door, blocking the road. During Alison's absence a queue of traffic had built up behind the van and several drivers were sounding their horns.

The other caller turned out to be an important client who was not used to being kept waiting and forcibly pointed this out to Roger Brownlee when he eventually did see him. Roger called Freda in and told her to "get Alison sorted out". Freda was very angry with Alison over the affair.

Week two

1 Week two did not start any better. A very smartly-dressed girl appeared and stated that she was expected for an interview. Alison pointed out that she knew nothing about the girl's arrival and asked her whom she had to see. The girl informed her that she was not certain but that the interview was for a word processing job. Alison contacted the general office and asked them if they knew anything about this. They assured her that they did not but that they would contact Freda, who presumably was scheduled to interview the girl.

Meanwhile Alison asked the girl to take a seat in a nearby empty office. About 45 minutes later the girl, whom Alison had forgotten about, approached the desk and said that she was leaving as she was not interested in working for such an inefficient firm. Freda, when she learned of the events, was furious with Alison for not making more effort to contact her.

46   Administrative Management Case Studies

2   Later that week a visitor arrived to speak to James Peters. Alison had just directed him to James's office when a second visitor arrived to see him. Alison was in the process of asking the second caller to wait while she contacted James Peters, when the telephone rang. It was an angry client who refused to believe that Alison was unable to find Roger Brownlee. When he eventually rang off, Alison was very upset since she had not known how to handle the situation. She then suddenly spotted James Peter's second visitor and realised that there was no empty chair on which he could have sat down. The chair which was there was piled high with booklets which had just arrived from the printers.

Alison was just trying to clear the chair when the telephone rang again. By the time that she had dealt with the call she realised that James Peter's visitor was showing considerable signs of impatience. Alison eventually got him seated to wait until James Peters was free, but not before he pointed out that he had already been waiting for almost 25 minutes.

It was at this point that she discovered that the second visitor had an appointment with James Peters. (She later learned that the first visitor, whom she had sent along to James's office without informing him, had not had an appointment. He had in fact been a salesman trying to sell a new computer program to the practice.) James Peters had been furious at being "landed" with the salesman while the visitor with the appointment was kept standing about.

ACTION

1   Identify the problems highlighted in the case study.

2   To what extent do you feel that the problems in Brownlee & Smith are caused by Alison's ignorance and inefficiency?

3   If a consultant had been called in to investigate the situation in the reception area, write the report which might have been presented to management highlighting where the organisational systems had been at fault and recommending changes which should be introduced.

Case 4.2
Appointments and diary management

General objectives: To gain an understanding of problems which can arise in appointments and diary management

To analyse the case and recommend solutions

To document acceptable administrative procedures

Skills developed: Analysis
Problem-solving
Decision-making
Documenting procedures
Communication

WESTFIELD ADVERTISING AGENCY (1)

Background

The Westfield Advertising Agency is a medium-sized private company with its headquarters in Carlisle and five smaller offices in other towns in the north of England. The agency has been in existence for 74 years and Henry Westfield, the Managing Director, is the third generation of the family to manage the business. He and 43 other full-time employees are located in Carlisle.

Over the past few years, the agency has been experiencing a cash flow crisis resulting from a drop in the number of clients with no offsetting increase in the average size of account. The Board of Directors had expressed some concern that the public image of the agency was of a rather old-fashioned organisation. After much discussion, the Directors decided to create a new post of Public Relations Officer to improve the public image of the agency and to co-ordinate efforts to break into new areas of advertising.

Four months ago, Angela Crowley, who is young, dynamic and very persuasive, was appointed to the new post. Because of the financial situation, Henry Westfield reluctantly agreed that Angela should receive secretarial support from Mary Maxwell, his Personal Assistant. It was felt that Mary would be able to take on this further responsibility because both Henry and Angela would be away quite a lot, and Mary had previously had some spare time which she had

48 Administrative Management Case Studies

often used to help the two Word Processing Operators when they were particularly pressurised.

Problems

1 Henry has been angry with Mary over two appointments which she had arranged for him. With the first one she had omitted to tell him until the morning in question that she had agreed to a journalist coming at 10.30 am to interview him. The journalist was wishing to write an article on the imminent "75th birthday" of the agency for a future edition of a leading monthly magazine. When he found out, Henry had asked Mary to telephone the journalist and postpone the appointment. This had not proved to be possible as the journalist had not left his telephone number. As a result Henry had to spend much of the morning with him.

This caused Henry major problems as he had counted on having that time to prepare an important paper about which he had suddenly remembered the night before. The paper had been called for at the last Director's Meeting and Henry knew that all papers for the next Director's Meeting *had* to be sent out that day.

2 The second problem involved a clash of appointments. Two afternoons later, while Henry was in a meeting, Mary had taken a telephone call from Sir Reginald Compton (one of the agency's most important clients who had recently had cause for complaint about poor quality of service). He asked if he could come and see Henry at 10 am on the following morning (Wednesday) and Mary, having checked her diary to see that Henry was free at that time, arranged the appointment. Since Henry's meeting lasted much longer than expected, Mary had not seen him before she left on the Tuesday to tell him of the arrangement for the next morning. She had put a note in his in-tray but, because he had been in a rush to get away after the meeting, he had not looked at the tray.

3 Unfortunately, unknown to Mary, Henry had planned to be out of town on the Wednesday. She only learned of this when she reached the office the next morning and he did not arrive. Remembering the 10 am appointment, Mary telephoned his home and was told by his wife that he had gone to Workington that day. (When she next saw Henry, he pointed out that he had arranged the visit at the end of the previous week and that it was entered in his own diary.) Mary realised that Sir Reginald Compton would already have left his home near Keswick and that she would be unable to stop him. When he arrived and found that Henry was out all day, he had been extremely displeased and this had not improved the already strained relationship between the two men.

4 Later on that Wednesday, the trade union representative had called demanding to see Henry on Thursday at 9 am to have a preliminary discussion on the management proposals for a new job evaluation scheme. In some confusion, Mary noted that Henry was involved with the Personnel Officer in a recruitment interview panel from 9.30 to 11.30 am. She reluctantly agreed to the appointment, however, on the insistence of the union official. When Henry

arrived at 9.10 am on the Thursday, he was furious to learn of the events of the previous day and to find the union official impatiently waiting for him outside his door.

5 Angela was also furious with Mary. On her way out of the office one day, she had requested Mary to telephone a potential client, Mrs Jennifer Croft, and ask if it would be convenient for Angela to call and see her the following Friday at 11 am. Angela had told Mary to leave her a note if the time was unsuitable. When she arrived at Mrs Croft's office the next week, she found that Mrs Croft was on holiday and her secretary was very insistent that Mary had never telephoned. On Angela's return to the office, Mary had looked back in her diary and found the entry, telling her to telephone, among the notes made the previous week. She pointed out that she had been very busy that day and had not had time to telephone, but admitted that she had then forgotten all about it.

Electronic diary management

The issue of diary management was one of the topics in a discussion Henry had with Angela. They both were annoyed about the problems they had experienced recently. The following week Angela went to Henry with the proposal that they introduce a system of electronic diary management like that which a friend of hers had recently installed in her own organisation. Angela's friend reported that it seemed to be bringing a significant improvement to the organisation. Henry expressed interest in the idea and suggested that they find out more about it.

ACTION

1 Identify the problems highlighted in the above case study.

2 Examine the issues which these problems raise.

3 Suggest what Mary should have done to avoid the problems occurring.

4 Draw up a list of procedures which should be followed when

  a arranging appointments and
  b managing a diary

5 Examine the extent to which the use of electronic diary management software would have resolved the problems experienced by Westfield? Give reasons for your answer.

Case 4.3
Time management, working relationships and administrative procedures

General objectives: To gain an understanding of some of the problems which can arise in managing time and in working for more that one person

To identify problem areas in administration

To develop an understanding of the role of the secretary as a member of a team

To analyse the case and recommend solutions

Skills developed: Analysis
Problem-solving
Decision-making

WESTFIELD ADVERTISING AGENCY (2)

Background

The Westfield Advertising Agency is a medium-sized, private company with its headquarters in Carlisle and five smaller offices in other towns in the north of England. The agency has been in existence for 74 years and Henry Westfield, the Managing Director, is the third generation of the family to manage the business. He and 43 other full-time employees are located in Carlisle.

Over the past few years, the agency has been experiencing a cash flow crisis resulting from a drop in the number of clients, with no offsetting increase in the average size of account. The Board of Directors had expressed some concern that the public image of the agency was of a rather old-fashioned organisation. After much discussion, the Directors decided to create a new post of Public Relations Officer to improve the public image of the agency and to co-ordinate efforts to break into new areas of advertising.

Four months ago, Angela Crowley, who is young, dynamic and very persuasive, was appointed to the new post. Because of the financial situation, Henry reluctantly agreed that Angela should receive secretarial support from Mary Maxwell, his Personal Assistant. It was felt that Mary would be able to take on this further responsibility because both Henry and Angela would be away quite a lot, and Mary had previously had some spare time which she had often used to help the Word Processing Operators when they were particularly pressurised.

Difficulty in time management

Things went reasonably smoothly for Mary for the first month of Angela's appointment. After that, however, problems started to build up and she found it increasingly difficult to get through all the work demanded of her. The workload from Henry seemed to be increasing in quantity and in the degree of urgency. Angela, who regularly was out of the office, often worked at home in the evening and called into the office early the next morning before Mary had arrived, leaving work for her on her desk. It was normal for this work also to be marked "urgent". On the days Angela was out of the office she frequently returned in the late afternoon and once again presented Mary with a number of items to be typed immediately.

Mary experienced great difficulty both in coping with the amount of work given to her and in prioritising the different material she received. She discussed the problem with Angela, who indicated that there was no way that the workload could be reduced nor given to Mary any earlier because Angela had so much to do and so many different people to see.

Conflict in working relationships

Henry rather resented the fact that Mary was not always available to do his work. Conflict had occurred on several occasions when he had "pulled rank" and demanded that Mary leave the work she was producing for Angela and undertake some work for him. Angela was very annoyed and on one occasion lost her temper, saying that the delay had resulted in a deadline being missed and the chance of some new business being lost. On that occasion the document Henry wanted typed was an after dinner speech he was to give later that week at the annual dinner of the golf club of which he was President. Mary was very upset by the whole situation as she felt that she was caught between her two bosses and had little chance of pleasing either.

Problems with administrative procedures

It seemed to Mary that nothing was going smoothly. She had forgotten to pass on an important verbal message to Henry which one of the staff had given to her in the corridor on her way to the General Office. Henry had also been annoyed when Mary had asked for another filing cabinet to store Angela's files. He pointedly replied that there was plenty of space in some of the cabinets already there. He was further annoyed when Mary mentioned that Angela wanted to centralise the records for the entire organisation. He commented that new staff should "learn a thing or two about the organisation before trying to revolutionise it".

The records themselves also concerned Mary. Because she had been so busy, a tremendous backlog had built up of material waiting to be filed. On two occasions this had resulted in Henry not having a vital paper for a meeting. He had been annoyed on the first occasion and furious when it happened a second time a few days later. He had ordered Mary to get the filing done, but so far she had not managed to find time to do it.

She was also concerned that she could not find an important document which Angela had given her to pass to Henry. Mary remembered putting it to one side, intending to give it to Henry when he came into the office, but she could not find it a few days later among any of the heaps of paper on her desk. She could only think that it had got mixed up with some other papers she had on her desk at the time although she could not rule out the possibility that she had inadvertently thrown it out. This would certainly appear to have happened with an address she had noted down on the back of an envelope during a telephone conversation.

ACTION

1 Identify the problems highlighted in the case study.

2 What, in your opinion, are the causes (obvious and underlying) of the problems?

3 Given the assumption that it is not possible to employ more administrative/secretarial staff, recommend steps which should be taken to improve the situation.

Case 4.4
Travel arrangements

General objectives: To reinforce learning on the procedures for arranging travel

To gain an understanding of some of the problems which can occur when making travel arrangements

To identify the causes of any problems

To draw up a checklist for arranging travel

Skills developed: Analysis
Problem-solving
Decision-making
Documenting procedures
Communication

THE EUSTON FILM COMPANY LTD

Background

The Euston Film Company is a fairly new and growing company in the film business. Most of its work is involved with producing films and videos for industrial companies. In the last few years, however, Euston has extended into the area of advertising and has landed one or two excellent contracts.

The demands of the business require the management and film crews to undertake quite a lot of travelling - some of it overseas. Making travel arrangements is therefore an important part of the work of the Personal Assistant to the Finance Officer.

New Personal Assistant

Brian Davies, the Finance Officer, has just appointed a new Personal Assistant, Harry Todd. At his interview Harry had discussed his considerable previous experience as Personal Assistant in two companies. Brian was delighted to get someone like Harry as he had experienced some difficulty in replacing his previous Personal Assistant, who had been with him for 11 years.

One of the first jobs given to Harry was to make travel arrangements for Brian, who was going to a one-day conference in Edinburgh on the Tuesday after next. Brian informed Harry that he was having a golfing weekend with a friend at Turnberry immediately before the Tuesday in question and, since he was travelling to Turnberry in his friend's car, he would like Harry to arrange transport for him to get from Turnberry to Edinburgh on the Monday. Harry was also asked to book a hotel for Monday and Tuesday nights, to arrange appointments for Brian to see two potential clients in Edinburgh on Wednesday and to book him on to the London train later that day. Brian indicated that he would be away for the next two days and would get the details from Harry when he returned.

Harry did not admit to Brian that he had never been asked to make travel arrangements before. He set to, however, and was very pleased at the speed and ease with which he got the arrangements made. Brian was a day later than he had said in returning due to an unforeseen problem which had arisen. He also arrived back to a minor crisis in the film company and did not have time to discuss the arrangements about the travel with Harry. He merely inquired if Harry had managed to get everything worked out. Brian did not mention the travel again until the Friday morning just before he was leaving for Turnberry. He had only time to grab the folder Harry had ready for him and to say that Harry should contact him if any major crises arose.

Travel arrangements for a film crew

While Brian was away for the three days, Harry was asked to make travel arrangements for a film crew to fly to New York to undertake an urgent assignment. He contacted the travel agent with whom the company normally dealt and asked them to book three people on the flight to New York in two days' time.

Brian's return

When Brian returned from Scotland he called Harry into his office. It was clear to Harry that Brian was not pleased and when Harry asked how his trip had gone, Brian could barely control his temper. It appeared that the trip had been something of a disaster.

After spending much of the Monday on the golf course, Brian had got a taxi from Turnberry to Ayr, from where he caught the train to Glasgow. He realised from the itinerary that Harry had given him that, once there, he had not a lot of time to catch the Edinburgh train. What he had not bargained for, and neither had Harry, was that the Ayr train came into Glasgow Central Station and the next Edinburgh train out of Central Station did not leave for an hour and a half. Earlier trains to Edinburgh left from Glasgow Queen Street Station. By the time Harry discovered this and got to Queen Street he had missed the next train to Edinburgh. Brian had no trouble catching the subsequent train. What he found annoying was that instead of taking 50 minutes it took an hour and, unlike the trains from Central Station which were InterCity trains, did not have any catering facilities. Apart from being very irritating, the situation had not been a disaster as Brian had reached Edinburgh on the Monday - if somewhat later than he had expected!

Arrival at the hotel

The problems had begun again when he reached the hotel and found that they did not appear to have reserved a room for him. They checked through their records but found nothing. One of the receptionists did, however, think that she remembered receiving a telephone call asking about accommodation but was fairly certain that it had not been a definite booking. She said she remembered particularly because the caller had said he was from a film company. They certainly had no record of any contact since then. As it happened, they did have a room free, although it was a much smaller room than Brian would have liked.

The conference hotel, he discovered, was within easy walking distance of where he was staying. When he rose on Tuesday it was raining very heavily but, because of the proximity of the conference hotel, he decided that it would be silly to take a taxi. He was, however, annoyed at getting wet and cast envious eyes at those attending the conference who only had to come downstairs from their rooms.

The Wednesday appointments

The first appointment on Wednesday went very well to start with and looked like resulting in interesting and lucrative work for the film company. Unfortunately the meeting over-ran by 45 minutes and Brian realised that he was already half an hour late for his next appointment.

He asked for a taxi to be called and, while he was waiting for it to arrive, he got out his itinerary card to find the address. It was with considerable annoyance that he realised that the address had been missed off the card. At that point the taxi arrived and Brian asked the driver if he knew the location of the firm. The taxi driver indicated that he did and so they set off. The traffic was very heavy but they made reasonable time. Unfortunately when he reached the firm Brian found that Anne Halliday, whom he was due to see, was located in another building some distance away.

By the time he reached the second building he was over an hour late. Brian's frustration increased when he learned that Anne had had to go to another meeting. Since she would not be free for the rest of the day she had asked her Assistant, Madge, to see Brian. Madge had been as helpful as she could be and certainly took the information for Anne. Unfortunately, however, she did not have the knowledge or authority to deal with the matter and so Brian felt it had been rather a wasted visit.

The London train

Brian had not enjoyed his journey back to London. He managed to reach Waverley Station just before the train left and was glad that he had a booked seat as the train was packed. He was, however, annoyed to find that he was not travelling first class as he usually did. When he located his seat, he was even more annoyed to find that he was not in an "airline" seat, that he had a woman with two noisy young children beside him and his back was to the engine. He consoled himself with the thought that he could spend quite a lot of the journey in the restaurant car. That train, however, did not have a restaurant car - only a buffet!

The film crew's arrival in New York

The film crew's trip to New York had been beset by problems also. Harry, in his hurry, had asked for sterling travel cheques which the film crew found much less convenient than dollar cheques would have been. They had had to spend some considerable time going to a bank to get them changed instead of being able to use them like money in shops and restaurants.

When they had arrived in New York the crew had gone to pick up their hired car, only to find that one had not been booked for them. Fortunately, they had managed to hire one on the spot although it did cost the organisation more that it would have done had it been hired and paid for in the UK.

Communication with London

During the visit it became clear to the film crew that they urgently required some financial information which they could only get from Brian. They telephoned him to discuss the matter but could only get Harry as Brian was in an important management meeting. Harry agreed to leave a memo for Brian to send the information late that afternoon when he returned from the meeting. Unfortunately the meeting lasted much longer that anticipated and did not finish until almost 9 pm in the evening. When Brian returned to his office to pick up his coat, he noticed the memo from Harry. He quickly got the information together, knowing that because of the time difference a fax would still get the information there on time. He was furious when he found out that Harry had not recorded the New York fax number. He tried telephoning the crew but could not get through since the switchboard had closed down for the night.

Damage to camera equipment

The final straw came when one of the cameras was damaged during the plane journey home. The crew and Brian were annoyed but not too worried as they knew they would get insurance money. Subsequent investigation revealed that this was not the case since special insurance had not been taken out for the camera equipment.

ACTION

1 Read the case study and identify any good or bad practices related to the making of travel arrangements.

2 In your opinion, what were the causes of the travel problems experienced by the Euston Film Company?

3 Did you identify any other problems highlighted by the case? If so, what were they and what were their causes.

4 Draw up a general checklist for arranging travel which could be given to Harry or anyone else in a similar position in any organisation.

SECTION 5
INFORMATION MANAGEMENT

Information is the cornerstone of the organisation. The importance of information to the survival of a business is recognised by the use of the term "information revolution" to describe the momentous changes which have taken place in the industrial world since the 1970s.

The introduction of the early computers produced a significant increase in the quantity of data available to managers in making decisions. Arguably, however, data only becomes "information", and of use in decision-making, when it is processed/managed and produced in a form which is meaningful to the decision-maker. Managing information has always presented problems for an organisation but the widespread use of computer technology presents particular problems to today's Manager. Computer technology has not only increased the quantity of information available; it has also changed market conditions for most organisations. Speedy and accurate information can be a vital factor in the securing of orders in an increasingly international market. There has therefore been an growing recognition of the importance of effective processing and management of information - the area that is now becoming known as information management.

Information takes many forms - written, verbal, aural, visual or tactile. The majority of business information either originates in written form or is subsequently produced in written form which may be text, data or graphics, or any combination of these three. Information is inextricably linked with administration in that before any administration can take place there must be a flow of information. Information is also an inherent part of every aspect of administration (eg organisational structure cannot be designed without information, human resources cannot be managed without information flow and information is vital to the management of change).

This section examines some of the key issues in information management - the effective recording of information, the effective presentation of information and the efficient management of the subsequent records/database. Considerable attention to the efficient recording of information is given in other sections of this book and in particular in Sections 3 and 4. This section, however, examines the importance of establishing, documenting and publicising procedures to enable the correct information to be conveyed to the correct destination at the correct time.

The presentation of information to management in a form which aids decision-making is an area of information management which is growing in importance with the increase in the volume of data and the development of sophisticated software for effective document presentation. Part of this section takes a brief look at one aspect of the presentation of information - namely the presentation of statistical information.

Perhaps the most important issue in information management is the management of records. This has always been an area of concern for organisations but it is one which has become more complex as the quantity of records increases along with the need for more speedy access to these records. Computerisation has added to, and complicated, the problem for Records Managers and part of this section examines some of the issues involved in records management.

Case 5.1
Records management

General objectives: To identify good practice in records management

To gain an understanding of problems which can arise if good practice is not present

Skills developed: Analysis
Problem-solving
Decision-making

ROYAL HOSPITAL (1)

Background

Royal Hospital is a fairly large hospital, situated in a large city, which deals mainly with orthopaedic and geriatric cases. As in most hospitals, there are a number of special units, one of which is Dietetics. The staff in the unit is as follows:

Janet Hall - Chief Dietician
Robert Webb - Senior Dietician (Diabetics)
Anne Fleming - Senior Dietician (Renal)
Joan Barr - Basic Grade Dietician
2 other Basic Grade Dieticians

In recent months the unit has been under considerable pressure, with an increasing number of patients. There have also been staff changes during the period - Anne Fleming is new to Dietetics, having come from a large hospital in another Health Board; Joan Barr has only recently qualified.

Several problems have recently become obvious in the unit and a number of these are related to records management. Although the main patient records are kept in the hospital centralised system, the unit requires to handle a substantial number of records. It has card files, using the alphabetical system, for its patients and general files (also in alphabetical order) for other records. In addition, the unit requires to keep a record of petty cash, information on all orders sent and detailed statistics on patient turnover.

Dietetics Unit

1 Anne Fleming had been rather horrified to find that there was no clerical support for the Dietetics Unit and had experienced considerable frustration at the time it was taking her to find the cards for some of her patients. After investigation she realised that the card files contained the records for all patients from the last 15 years. On suggesting to Janet Hall that someone needed to sort through the cards and get rid of all the old ones, she was firmly told that they required to keep past records and that this unit was not as fortunate as her last one in having modern records equipment and clerical support. Anne retorted that if the unit records of patient turnover had been properly kept Janet would probably have been able to make a case to the management for the allocation of clerical help. Janet was furious at what she interpreted as a personal criticism of her ability to manage the unit.

2 Joan Barr had been nearby at the time and had overheard the comments. At lunch, during a conversation with Anne, she said that she had worked during some of her holidays in a large company where they used a numerical system because of the number and turnover of records. She said it had operated very well and they were able to find the records quickly. She thought it would improve the situation in the unit as all the recent record cards would have the highest numbers. Anne was not too clear about the numerical system but said she would try to find out a bit more and, if it was going to help, would tackle Janet again.

3 Anne was also frustrated at the fact that Robert Webb never seemed to do his share of maintaining the record cards. She regularly tried to keep up to date those that referred to the renal patients and had also spent time on five occasions in the last month in clearing the backlog of the others. She had hoped that this would encourage (or shame) Robert into doing his share but this had not happened. Later that same day Anne was complaining to Robert about the backlog which had once again built up. He gave no appearance of being very concerned and merely blamed the lack of clerical support. In desperation, Anne loudly announced that she was not doing his work any more and was going to get a separate box for the renal cards which she would then keep up-to-date. Robert replied that this would not work as there were a number of patients with both renal and diabetic problems. Anne grew even more angry.

4 The strained relationships in the unit were further aggravated the following day when Anne had occasion to telephone one of the renal consultants to discuss the implications of a new medication for a patient in the renal ward. During the conversation Anne realised that she required the relevant medication file to be able to discuss the issue in depth. She put the phone down to get the file out of the cabinet only to find that it was not there. She searched through the piles on each person's desk but still did not find it, by which time the consultant had given up waiting and had rung off. He was not pleased when Anne telephoned again to postpone the remainder of the discussion until she had located the file. He made some very pointed remarks on the importance of public image and the poor impression of efficiency created by leaving someone waiting on the telephone and by losing files. It was not until late in the afternoon, after much searching and asking around,

that Anne discovered that Janet had taken the file home and forgotten to return it.

5   When Janet saw Anne publicly make a grimace on learning of the whereabouts of the file, she called her into a room and reprimanded her for her attitude and behaviour, particularly when there was every chance of one of the patients witnessing the scene. She further pointed out that she had already received a criticism from a patient about Anne's argument with Robert the previous day.

ACTION

1   Analyse the case and identify problems related to records management.

2   What are the causes of the problems and how could they have been avoided?

3   Can you identify any other problems which have aggravated the records management problems? How could these have been overcome.

Case 5.2
Records management and general administrative procedures

General objectives: To identify good practice in records management

To gain an understanding of problems which can arise if good practice is not present

To gain an insight into the complex nature of any organisational problem

To draw up a set of guidelines

Skills developed: Analysis
Problem-solving
Decision-making
Documenting procedures
Communication

ROYAL HOSPITAL (2)

Background

Royal Hospital is a fairly large hospital situated in a large city dealing mainly with orthopaedic and geriatric cases. As in most hospitals there are a number of special units, two of which are Dietetics and Occupational Therapy. The staff of the Occupational Therapy unit is as follows:

Alison Anderson - Chief Occupational Therapist
2 Senior Occupational Therapists
George Croft - Basic Grade Occupational Therapist
Freda Norris - Basic Grade Occupational Therapist (part-time)
5 Basic Grade Occupational Therapists (4 full-time, 1 part-time)
Rachel McLeod - Receptionist/Clerical Assistant

In recent months both units have been under considerable pressure with an increasing number of patients. There have also been several staff changes in Occupational Therapy during the period - Freda Norris has recently joined the staff on a part-time basis and Rachel McLeod has transferred from the post of

Clerical Assistant on one of the wards. She was particularly welcome since the post had been vacant for four months.

Several problems have recently become obvious in the two units and a number of these are related to records management. Although the main patient records are kept in the hospital's centralised system, the units require to handle a substantial number of their own records. They both have card files, using the alphabetical system, for their patients, and general files (also in alphabetical order) for other records. In addition, the units require to keep a record of petty cash, information on all orders sent and detailed statistics on patient turnover.

Occupational Therapy Unit

1. The Occupational Therapy Unit was not without its troubles. The staff had suffered very much during the four months' vacancy period. Mary, the previous Receptionist/Clerical Assistant, had had "her own system" for recording equipment and for dealing with loans to patients. The Occupational Therapists, who had to undertake all the clerical work during the vacancy, had found the system difficult to understand and rather time-consuming.

   As a result when Rachel, the new Receptionist, tried to carry out an inventory of the equipment, there appeared to be a considerable amount missing. A number of the staff remembered to whom some of the items had been loaned. Rachel subsequently made a start on trying to get the equipment returned. A few patients whom she contacted were upset by the request and one was irate. They all maintained that they had been promised the loan of the equipment for a longer period and the irate patient stated that she did not see why she was now being "hounded".

   Rachel discussed the situation with Alison Anderson and it was agreed that Rachel should take no further action for a few weeks even if this meant that no reminder was sent to some patients who had considerably overdue equipment.

2. A further problem arose when Rachel tried to balance the petty cash. A meeting of the staff resulted in the identification of the "missing money". It appeared that two purchases had not been recorded in the petty cash book. Both involved the part-timer, Freda Norris, who had taken some money to buy urgently required materials. She said that she had left a note on the desk indicating what she had done, since she was unsure how and where to record this. Further investigation brought to light that the note had been written on a scrap of paper, that the desk had already been covered with sundry piles of paper and that the receipts were still in Freda's handbag. The meeting also identified that some receipts from other staff were missing. A hunt in the back of one of the desk drawers brought to light three missing, crumpled receipts. Alison asked Rachel as a priority to tighten up and, if necessary, change the unit's record systems.

General

1 A problem arose with an important meeting of all the units called by a senior member of the hospital management. Neither Alison Anderson nor Robert Webb arrived. Considerable time was lost in trying to locate them. Robert was eventually tracked down in one of the hospital wards. He confessed to having forgotten to look at his diary for that day. Rachel, the unit Receptionist/Clerical Assistant, said that she had no idea where Alison was but that, since she had not seen her all day, she assumed that Alison must be out on a visit somewhere. Alison's own diary was missing. Subsequent investigation revealed that she was visiting one of the other city hospitals and had taken her diary with her.

2 The previous week a general circular had been sent out to all departments and units stating that the hospital management team was hoping to extend computerisation and that in a year's time, if everything went according to plan, there would be a microcomputer terminal in each of the units. It was stated that a computerised database would be one of the first items to be considered. The circular caused a mixed response in both units. A number of the staff were very apprehensive, one or two were positively hostile, while others' reactions ranged from interested to enthusiastic.

ACTION

1 Analyse this second part of the case on the Royal Hospital (ie following on from Case 5.1) and identify the problems.

2 What are the causes of the problems and how could they have been avoided?

3 Using the information from the two parts of the case study (ie Cases 5.1 and 5.2), draw up a set of guidelines on records management which, in future, could be given to any new employee who is required to handle records.

Case 5.3
Business documentation

General objectives: To identify the various procedures involved in one aspect of a sales transaction

To document the process of a transaction in the form of a flow chart

To examine the implications of computerisation

Skills developed: Analysis
Problem-solving
Decision-making
Creating a flow chart

PATERSON & BROWN PLC (1)

Background

In an attempt to improve efficiency, the Efficiency Audit Section of Paterson & Brown plc, a manufacturing company, has been carrying out a detailed examination of the work flow within the Sales Department. One section of the work of the department is the handling of orders.

Order process

The organisation has five Sales Representatives, each assigned to a different geographical area. The mail within the Sales Department is opened by the Office Junior and the orders from the Representatives are passed to a Clerk for checking to ensure that each order is correctly completed. If any piece of information has been omitted or incorrectly recorded, the Clerk has to decide whether he can rectify the error or omission himself or whether he requires to contact the appropriate Sales Representative.

The Clerk subsequently checks the creditworthiness of the client before sanctioning the order. If there is a problem and a stop has been put on further credit to that customer, the Clerk will return the order to the Sales Representative to take up the matter with the customer. The Clerk then sorts the acceptable orders into the five areas and passes them to the relevant Invoice Clerk.

There are two Invoice Clerks, one dealing with the two largest areas and the other with the three smaller areas. They create an invoice for each order, a copy of which is passed to the Stores Department for checking that the goods are in stock. When the response from the Stores is received, the invoice is recalled and any necessary amendments are made and the totals extended. The invoices are processed in batches and copies are then sent to the different departments for further processing. The Invoice Clerks pass the total of each batch to the Senior Clerk in the Sales Department, who collates the information and produces total sales figures for the Department, along with a breakdown of the sales figures for each Representative.

ACTION

1 Identify the procedures involved in the handling of an order within the Sales Department of Paterson & Brown plc.

2 Document these procedures in the form of a flow chart.

3 Analyse the information in the case and examine how computerisation could reduce the work and improve efficiency in Paterson & Brown plc. Produce the flow chart for the improved order process which would result from the introduction of your computerisation programme.

Case 5.4
Statistical presentation

General objectives: To analyse a series of statistics

To determine the best method of graphical presentation to meet a range of management requirements

To use spreadsheet software to design a system to provide management information

To construct a range of graphical presentations to improve the quality of management information

Skills developed: Analysis
Problem-solving
Decision-making
Constructing graphical charts manually and electronically
Spreadsheet design

PATERSON & BROWN PLC (2)

Background

Paterson & Brown plc is a small manufacturing company which sells its products through five Sales Representatives, each of whom is assigned to a different geographical area. The Representatives receive a monthly salary which is supplemented by a quarterly bonus if they exceed the sales targets set by the organisation. Every month the Senior Clerk of the Sales Department collates the sales statistics for the department as a whole and for each of the five Representatives. At the end of every quarter the quarterly sales of each Representative are compared with his/her sales target and the information presented to the Sales Manager for calculation of any bonuses.

Current problem

Comments were made by senior management to the Sales Manager, at the beginning of a new financial year, that his department was not operating at maximum efficiency. They indicated that there were two areas requiring attention.

The first of these was the need for an improvement in the speed and effectiveness of his decision-making. This, they felt, was of particular importance given the competition they were facing from other organisations. The second area they highlighted was the need to increase the productivity of the Sales Representatives in general and of some of them in particular. They indicated that the Sales Manager should work towards increasing the targets for each Representative.

Proposed solution

After a discussion with a friend, who occupies a similar post in another organisation, the Sales Manager decided that one thing which would help improve the speed and effectiveness of his decision-making would be a more efficient presentation of the monthly and quarterly sales statistics. He also felt that this would increase the information available to the Sales Representatives and could be used in the campaign to increase productivity. He decided that the information should be presented in graphical form rather than in written or tabular form as at present. He therefore called in his Senior Clerk, who collates and processes the statistics, and discussed how best graphically to present the departmental statistics to provide the current information but, at the same time, to increase the general efficiency of the department.

He stated that he required:

1 to be able to compare at a glance the trends of the actual total sales with the target total sales over a period of six months;

2 to be able to compare the actual quarterly performance of any of the Representatives with his/her quarterly target;

3 to be able, each quarter, to provide each Representative with information on how his/her sales for that quarter compared with those of the other Representatives and with the quarterly sales as a whole.

The figures for the previous six months were as follows:

Sales Representative A

   Target sales = Jan £1200, Feb £1600, Mar £1700, Apr £1500, May £1400, June £1600

   Actual sales = Jan £1300, Feb £1500, Mar £1800, Apr £1700, May £1500, June £1800

Sales Representative B

   Target sales = Jan £2100, Feb £2300, Mar £2200, Apr £2100, May £2100, June £2400

   Actual sales = Jan £2100, Feb £2300, Mar £2100, Apr £2200, May £2200, June £2300

Sales Representative C

   Target sales = Jan £1500, Feb £1700, Mar £1600, Apr £1500, May £1600, June £1700

   Actual sales = Jan £1700, Feb £1600, Mar £1700, Apr £1700, May £1000, June £1600

Sales Representative D

Target sales = Jan £1300, Feb £1500, Mar £1700, Apr £1400, May £1500, June £1600

Actual sales = Jan £1500, Feb £1100, Mar £1400, Apr £1600, May £1600, June £1500

Sales Representative E

Target sales = Jan £2100, Feb £2200, Mar £2300, Apr £2000, May £2200, June £2400

Actual sales = Jan £2000, Feb £2300, Mar £2300, Apr £2200, May £2200, June £2400

ACTION

1 Analyse the case and decide which types of graphical presentation would best meet the stated requirements of the Sales Manager.

2 Produce manually an appropriate graph/chart to meet each of the stated requirements of the Sales Manager (ie produce a total of three graphs/charts).

3 Using a computer:

   a design a spreadsheet which will enable you to produce a series of graphical presentations to meet all of the stated requirements of the Sales Manager; and

   b produce appropriate graphs/charts to meet each of these requirements (ie produce a total of three graphs/charts).

SECTION 6
MEETINGS

Effective administration requires effective communication. One method of communication which is found in all types of organisation, regardless of size or the sector of the economy in which it is based, is meetings. Meetings can take many forms, varying from informal discussions among a small group of people to the highly structured and formal annual general meeting. Meetings cover topics ranging over the whole gamut of the work of an organisation and are therefore central to the functioning of any organisation.

This section will deal with formal meetings where there is a chairman and where minutes require to be produced. The amount of time taken up by such meetings varies from one organisation to another but, given that "time is money", all organisations where efficiency is a major goal, require to maximise the effectiveness of their meetings' procedure. It is surprising therefore, that so few organisations spend much time on training staff on meetings' procedure, the running of meetings, minute-taking and minute-writing.

The following section seeks to provide trainees with an understanding of the procedure at meetings, the technique of effective chairmanship and the skill required by the minute clerk. Since the skills of running a meeting and producing effective minutes are highly practical skills, the section concludes with some role-play exercises.

Case 6.1
Preparation for meetings

General objectives: To identify the duties relating to preparation for a meeting

To gain an understanding of some of the problems which can arise when there is inadequate preparation for meetings

To produce a set of guidelines on the procedure for meetings

Skills developed: Analysis
Problem-solving
Decision-making
Documenting procedures

THOMPSON ENTERPRISES PLC

Background

Thompson Enterprises is a fairly large company. As with most organisations, staff are involved in a substantial number of meetings. The duty of arranging and preparing for meetings is therefore very important but it is one for which training has never been provided by the organisation. Some members of staff who act as Meetings Clerks received training on meetings procedures as part of their basic administrative or secretarial training prior to joining the organisation. Others have gathered considerable experience over the years - often as a result of "trial and error".

Over the past few years, the organisation has been expanding and at the same time has lost quite a number of experienced Meetings Clerks through promotion or retirement. As a result, a number of new staff have been recruited, most of whom have only fairly limited experience of meetings.

Current problems

In recent months there have been many complaints about meetings, some of which are as follows:

1 A number of Chairpersons complained about poor attendance at meetings. Various reasons were given for this.

   a Some absentees indicated that they did not know anything about the meeting.

   b In a few cases members contacted the relevant Chairperson shortly after the meeting to apologise, stating that they had been away for two or three days. They had only realised that they had missed the meeting when they found the agenda in the mail on their return.

   c On two occasions a Chairperson had received angry telephone calls from three different committee members in response to a memo which had been sent out reminding them of their responsibility to attend meetings. The members all indicated that they had the meeting clearly scheduled in their diaries for the following week, which was the date which had been agreed at the previous meeting. The Chairperson pointed out that the change in date had occurred shortly after the meeting and that the new date had been given in both the minutes and the agenda. The members responded by demanding how they were to know that the date had been altered from that agreed at the meeting.

   d A similar problem had occurred over a meeting which was normally held in the afternoon but which, on this occasion, had been scheduled for the morning. Although no rescheduling had been involved, several members complained that they had not noticed that the time on the agenda was different from the normal time. At the same meeting the Chairperson had been annoyed by some members who arrived late and had then caused some disturbance in bringing in chairs for themselves.

2 After one Committee Meeting, two Managers were heard to moan about the slowness of the internal mail service as a paper for a meeting had taken more than a full day to get from one department to another. As a result it had not arrived in time for the meeting. A third Manager, John Black, added that at least they had got their paper - albeit late. His had never arrived this time and on a previous occasion his papers had been addressed to Jim Black who worked in another department. The problem of the two Managers had apparently been compounded by their not being able to get a photocopy of the paper at the meeting because of the Managing Director's memo about tightening up on the use of the photocopier in order to effect cost savings.

   Their moans were overheard by the Meetings Clerk. The next meeting of the Committee was due to be held on the tenth of the following month. On the ninth, the Meetings Clerk was given an important and lengthy paper by the Marketing Manager who was full of apologies for not getting it to the Clerk sooner. He stated that he had forgotten that he had been asked at the previous meeting to produce the paper. He had not remembered anything about it until he had been reading over the minutes the previous evening.

   Remembering the comments about the mail service and bearing in mind the continued restrictions on photocopying, the Meetings Clerk decided the only solution was to hand the paper out at the meeting. Although some sarcastic remarks were passed about the requirement in this company to possess speed-reading skills, the paper seemed to be well received as few people made comments. The Marketing Manager's recommendations were passed quite quickly.

One week later a furious argument broke out between the Production Manager and the Marketing Manager. The Production Manager stated that he had not realised the effect that the Marketing Manager's recommendations were going to have on his work schedules. The Marketing Manager pointed out very firmly that it had all been clearly spelled out in the paper. The Production Manager shouted a few rude remarks about the paper and stated that he was off to get the Chairperson to call a special meeting to examine the whole issue again and get some sensible decisions made. The Chairperson was not pleased when he heard about the situation.

3   There was also trouble regarding the Company's Annual General Meeting three weeks later. Confusion arose over the venue for the meeting, which was changed from the designated venue to a large meeting room in the Company's new building. A number of the Shareholders did not seem to have been notified of the change and arrived at the main building. Some time had been lost while the new receptionist on duty there had searched for someone to tell her where the meeting was being held. The Shareholders naturally were angry at the delay and inefficiency. The situation was not improved by the fact that some Shareholders "got lost" between the foyer of the new building and the relevant meeting room, despite following what they understood to be the directions given on the notice in the foyer. This had led to three Shareholders being late for the start of the meeting since they had already had major problems getting parked. Most of the parking spaces seemed to have been taken up by the company staff. The three Shareholders were very angry.

One of the senior Shareholders attending the Annual General Meeting wrote formally to the Managing Director about the waste of time at the meeting. Useful discussion on one matter had been held up for 10-15 minutes while the Minute Clerk had had to return to her office to look for a copy of a document relating to one of the important items under discussion. Further irritation occurred over the pieces of paper, circulating for most of the first half of the meeting, requesting Shareholders to sign their names to indicate their attendance at the meeting.

4   Complaints were also received about the Annual General Meeting of the Company's leisure club. A number of staff who had wanted to attend complained that the date had clashed with the regular monthly meeting of the Finance Committee and that, by the time they got notification of the Annual General Meeting, it was too late to make any alterations. The Meetings Clerk had strongly defended her position and said that, as a result of the earlier complaints, she had made sure that everyone had seven days' clear notice.

ACTION

1. Read the case study, identify the problems faced by Thompson Enterprises plc and analyse the causes.

2. What course of action would you recommend to solve the problems?

3. Prepare a set of guidelines which could be given to each Meetings Clerk on the procedure in the preparation for meetings.

Case 6.2
Effective meetings

General objectives: To gain an understanding of some of the factors which can reduce the effectiveness of meetings

To analyse the case and make recommendations

To gain skill in report writing

Skills developed:
Analysis
Problem-solving
Decision-making
Report-writing
Communication

CARLTON CREAMERIES PLC

Background

Carlton Creameries plc has recently been taken over by a large national food company which has indicated that it intends the company should be run as a subsidiary company with considerable autonomy. One thing which has been tightened up is the informality which was a hallmark of the Creameries prior to the takeover. As part of the takeover deal, and to keep some consistency, Albert West, the son of the former Managing Director of Carlton Creameries, has been appointed to be Managing Director of the new subsidiary. Albert has a lot of experience in finance and is ably supported by Alice Allen, the new Marketing Manager appointed by the Board of the parent company.

Albert's appointment has been generally welcomed as an excellent combination of the old and the new. It was a well known fact that Albert had had several serious disagreements with his father over financial management and he has already begun to introduce a considerable number of changes, not only in the financial area but also in other areas such as marketing, where new personnel have been introduced. A few of the older Managers who have been retained are unhappy about some of his ideas. One point about which there is general agreement and lack of enthusiasm is the way in which he chairs the monthly Board Meeting.

Albert, himself, has become concerned about the level of his meetings' skills. In an attempt to improve matters, he has invited a friend of his to come in and act as a Consultant - to sit in on some meetings and to report on the problems, making recommendations about how they can be resolved. The following is a resume of the two meetings which the Consultant attended.

The start of the meeting

The Consultant had been told that there should be about a dozen members attending the meeting. Two minutes before the meeting was due to start, when Albert and his Minute Clerk arrived, there were five other Managers in the room. Albert indicated, on taking his seat, that the majority of the other members would probably all be there in 5-10 minutes. It was fully 10 minutes before there was a quorum for the meeting and he decided that he could start.

Albert began by welcoming the Managers to the meeting. He stated that he was a bit concerned about the late start and hoped that everyone would make a greater effort to be on time for the next meeting so that he could get started a bit earlier. The apologies for absence were read and the minutes of the previous meeting approved fairly quickly. There were only two matters arising and these again were dealt with expeditiously.

The proposed new marketing strategy

Alice Allen was taken totally by surprise when Albert immediately asked her to speak to her paper on the proposed new marketing strategy. She asked Albert what had happened to the other items scheduled to be discussed before her paper. He replied that he thought it would be a good idea to take her paper now since the new Finance Director would no doubt want to take part in the discussion and could not stay until the end of the meeting. He also added that the Personnel Officer had not arrived yet and therefore could not give his paper, which was scheduled before Alice's paper. Alice talked to her paper, which had been circulated well before the meeting.

The discussion lasted for over an hour. At times it was very heated and at one point the Production Manager and Alice were shouting at each other. Albert got rather agitated. He hated the acrimony which so often developed between Managers and tried with no success to get the two of them to calm down. In the middle of the furore the Personnel Officer arrived. He asked the person next to whom he sat what the row was all about and then firmly interrupted Alice and the Production Manager, telling them to stop behaving like spoilt children. They were so taken aback that they stopped shouting. The Personnel Officer took the opportunity to talk about the need for harmony and synergy among the Managers and to tell them about the major improvement in the performance of a company, with which he had been associated for the past year, as a result of a team-building programme which had been followed over the period. By the time he had finished (some 10 minutes later) all the other members of the meeting had calmed down.

Further discussion followed, at the end of which Alice put a motion to the meeting that the company approve her new marketing strategy. This was seconded by the Finance Officer. The Production Manager immediately indicated that he was very unhappy about this. Albert asked him if he wished to put forward an amendment. The Production Manager said that he would like to put forward the amendment that they retain the existing strategy and discuss the matter again at the next meeting when they all would have had more time to suggest alternatives.

Albert announced that they would now vote on the motion and the amendment. He asked for a show of hands for Alice's motion. He then immediately asked for a show of hands for the Production Manager's amendment. He and the Minute Clerk counted the hands and the meeting was evenly divided. Albert indicated that he would give his casting vote to the motion put forward by Alice and announced that the new policy would be put into effect as soon as possible. There was a general outburst from those opposed to the motion who said that the vote was too close to make such a decision. Albert overruled them and reiterated that the policy would be introduced as soon as possible. He did, however, agree to review the situation in four months' time.

The remainder of the meeting

The meeting continued for another hour and a half with general and fairly protracted discussion on several issues.

When the time came for the Personnel Officer to speak, half of the members had left. The Personnel Officer introduced his Assistant, whom he had asked to be in attendance at the meeting to answer any questions on particular details of his paper. He then talked to his paper.

As a number of the remaining members obviously wanted to speak and time was running short, Albert indicated that there really was not time to ask the Assistant detailed questions and that those who wished to speak should try to be brief and would only be allowed to speak once. When the Personnel Officer tried to make some points in response to members' comments, Albert stopped him, saying that he had "had his turn" and that they would now vote on the motion. One of the members questioned whether the meeting was still quorate. Albert and the Minute Clerk had a brief discussion and stated that since the Personnel Officer had brought his Assistant along they had just the minimum number. The voting was quite clear with the Personnel Officer, his Assistant, Alice and two others voting for the motion. Albert announced that the motion had been carried and that all the staff would be informed of the decision before the end of the week.

As there was no other competent business, Albert thanked those who had stayed to the end and reminded them of the date of the next meeting.

ACTION

1 Analyse the case of Carlton Creameries and examine the problems which it highlights.

2 Identify where the case indicates that Carlton Creameries are deviating from the law and recognised procedure of meetings.

3 Taking the role of the Consultant, write the report you would submit to Albert West detailing the problems and making recommendations for their solution.

Case 6.3
Effective minutes (1)

General objectives: To identify factors which make for effective minutes of a meeting

To analyse the case and identify faults and causes

To gain practice in the skill of minute-writing

Skills developed: Analysis
Problem-solving
Decision-making
Minute-writing
Communication

BRITLAND HOME AND HEALTH DEPARTMENT (1)

Background

In the last two months, the Britland Home and Health Department (BHHD) has turned its attention to the recent Government directive on the need to improve care services for the elderly. An investigation into the Day Care provision for the elderly in Pentland Region is currently being carried out by Hamish Park, the Division Assistant Secretary. He initially made contact with Evelyn Proudfoot, Director of the Pentland Social Work Department, and established an Ad Hoc Committee to examine the issues and make recommendations on action which could be taken to improve the service.

Over the last four weeks Hamish has been corresponding with the General Manager of the Pentland Health Board, James Wilson, over veiled criticism that James has made of the Social Work Department. In his letters James has contended that the department requires to be put on a more "professional basis" but has not gone into any details of what the problem seems to be.

Hamish has spoken to Evelyn about the letters and received a tirade of complaints from her about there not being a problem other than interference on the part of James Wilson who, according to Evelyn, really wants to take over the Day Care service altogether. Evelyn also stated that she considered there was no need for the Health Board to be involved in the running of the Day Care Centres as the Social Work Department was perfectly capable of running the service and was quite prepared to call in any medical practitioners as and when required. Hamish decided not to pursue the matter further with Evelyn.

A few days later Hamish met two of the Pentland Social Workers who told him of a major personality clash between Evelyn and James Wilson. According to them, this was the crux of the problem. In his latest letter, James Wilson requested that the membership of the Ad Hoc Committee be extended to include himself and one of his medical colleagues with particular expertise in health care for the elderly.

Ad Hoc Committee Meeting

Hamish put the widening of the membership on the agenda of the next the Ad Hoc Committee Meeting. Since his regular Minute Clerk, John Clark, was unable to attend, Hamish, who was too busy to see Mary himself, asked one of his staff to get Mary Frame, a new Executive Officer in the Division, to come along to the meeting and take the minutes. (See chart on page 85 for those involved in this Ad Hoc Committee Meeting.)

At the meeting Hamish reported on the correspondence he had had with James Wilson and raised his request for the membership to be extended. Hamish suggested that, in his opinion, for the benefit of the service and for the good of future relations between the Social Work Department and the Health Board, the membership should be extended. He gave, as a further reason, his fear that the situation would deteriorate further and could well end up being reported in the newspapers. This would do no good for anyone and would badly damage the reputation of both the BHHD and, in particular, the Social Work Department.

At this point the meeting became acrimonious with Mrs Proudfoot, supported by her close friend, Victor Hamilton, taking strong exception to the suggestion and shouting at Janet Clarkson, who along with Tom Dean, was loud in her support of the proposal. A sixth member present at the meeting, Alec White, said very little. Hamish tried to reason with Evelyn to no avail and for a time the situation was one of stalemate while she "held forth" on the matter.

In an attempt to cool the atmosphere, Hamish finally appealed to Alec to give his opinion. With some trepidation Alec indicated that he favoured extending the membership to include the two members of the Health Board and suggested that perhaps Alison Morris, Warden of Forth Day Care Centre, the largest Day Care Centre in the region, could also be invited to attend in a non-voting capacity.

Hamish accepted the idea gladly and asked Alec to formulate both these points as a formal motion. This was supported by Janet. Seeing that she was about to be out-voted, Evelyn proposed an amendment, which was supported by Victor, that "membership from the Health Board should be confined to medical practitioners". The amendment fell, however, as only Evelyn and Victor supported it. After that the motion was passed on a vote of three to two and Hamish asked that the Minute Clerk should write to James Wilson and Alison Morris.

Minutes of the meeting

Mary Frame did not have an opportunity to have a discussion with Hamish after the meeting. She had found the meeting highly embarrassing, particularly as she had not expected any item to be controversial. The following is the minute which she drew up for the section of the Committee Meeting relating to the committee membership.

Extract of minute of the Ad Hoc Committee Meeting

4 COMMITTEE MEMBERSHIP

Mr Park told the meeting that he had received a letter from Mr James Wilson, General Manager of the Pentland Health Board, complaining about the Pentland Social Work Department, and that, on reply, he had received yet another letter stating that Mr Wilson would like to see the Day Care Centres put on a more professional basis. He had also asked that the committee membership be extended to include himself and a medical practitioner with particular expertise in care for the elderly. Hamish stated that he had contacted Evelyn who had said that there was no problem and had made a number of forceful points ending by stating that what James Wilson really wanted was to take over the Day Care service.

Hamish said that he had given the matter much thought and wished to propose that the membership should be extended because if this did not happen it might end up with the press being brought in, which would not be good for anyone and would be very harmful to the reputation of the Social Work Department.

Mrs Proudfoot was very angry and stated that under no circumstances would she agree to such a proposal. Mr Hamilton supported her while Mrs Clarkson supported Mr Park. Mr Dean also supported the idea of increasing the membership to include the two Health Board Representatives. A lot of heated discussion followed, with no agreement being reached. Hamish then asked Mr White for his opinion. Alec said that he was in favour of the proposal and would it not be helpful if Alison Morris, Warden of the largest Day Care Centre, was also invited. Hamish stated that he thought this was a good idea. He then changed his proposal to include that point and suggested that a vote should be taken. Further points were made but the outcome of the discussion and voting was that Hamish's proposal was carried.

BRITLAND HOME AND HEALTH DEPARTMENT (1)

The following is a chart showing those involved in the Ad Hoc Committee:

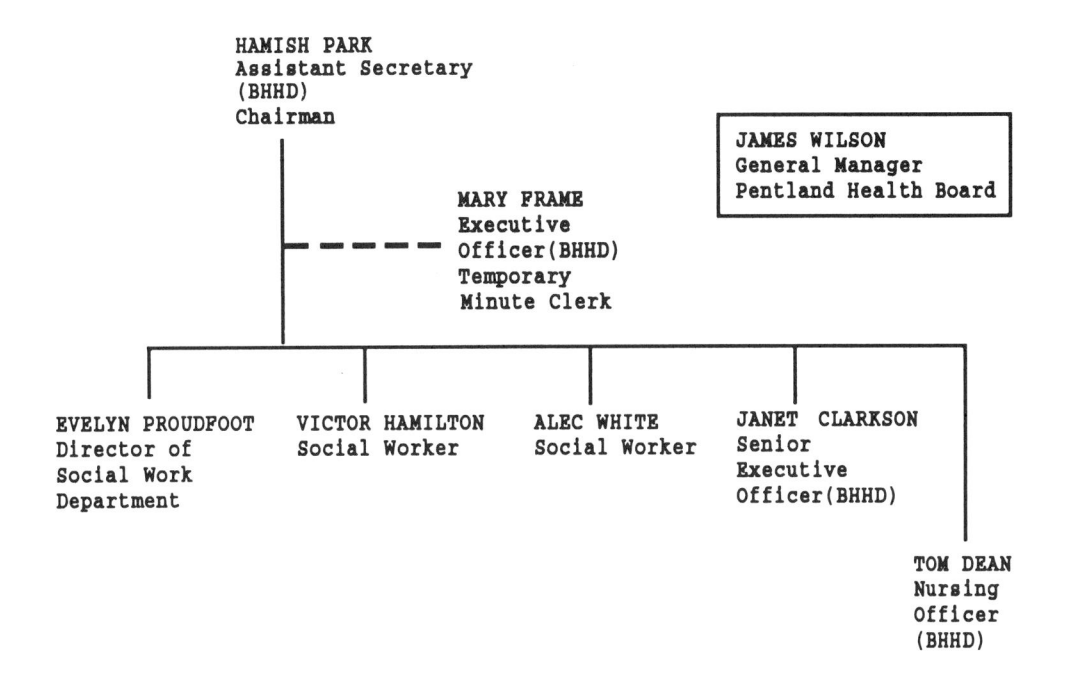

```
                    HAMISH PARK
                    Assistant Secretary
                    (BHHD)
                    Chairman                        JAMES WILSON
                         |                          General Manager
                         |      MARY FRAME          Pentland Health Board
                         |      Executive
                         |- - - Officer(BHHD)
                         |      Temporary
                         |      Minute Clerk
         _____|_____
         |           |            |            |
  EVELYN PROUDFOOT  VICTOR HAMILTON  ALEC WHITE   JANET CLARKSON
  Director of      Social Worker    Social Worker Senior
  Social Work                                     Executive
  Department                                      Officer(BHHD)
                                                        |
                                                  TOM DEAN
                                                  Nursing
                                                  Officer
                                                  (BHHD)
```

ACTION

You are asked to read the case study and answer the following:

1. Do you think the extract is a good minute of the discussion and action which took place at the meeting?

2. In your opinion, what criticism could be levelled at the minute and how could it have been improved?

3. Do you consider that Hamish Park could have improved matters by taking a different course of action? If so, what could he have done?

4. What other problems are likely to arise when taking notes at a meeting and when subsequently drawing up the minutes?

5. Draw up the minute which you would have written if you had been the Minute Clerk at that meeting.

Case 6.4
Effective minutes (2)

General objectives: To give practice in the skill of minute writing

Skills developed: Analysis
Decision-making
Minute-writing
Communication

BRITLAND HOME AND HEALTH DEPARTMENT (2)

Part 1 of the case study (Case 6.3) examined item 4 on the agenda of a meeting of the Ad Hoc Committee held on 31 October at 1430 hours in the Britland Offices. The earlier part of the meeting had gone fairly well. There was a full turn-out of members.

The first item on the agenda was the minutes of the previous meeting which had been held on 17 October at 1430 hours in the Britland Offices. Victor Hamilton pointed out that he had submitted apologies which had not been noted. Subject to that amendment, the minutes were approved.

Matters arising

The second item on the agenda was "Matters arising". There was only one "Matter arising" which related to the proposal, approved at the previous meeting, to conduct a survey of the range and extent of the Day Care Services for the elderly throughout the region. The Chairman reported that two members of staff from the local Polytechnic had been commissioned to undertake the survey. He indicated that the report was due for submission on 23 November.

Evelyn asked for assurance that the report would be submitted to the first meeting of the Ad Hoc Committee after the submission date (ie on 28 November). Hamish pointed out that, since the report had been commissioned by the Britland Home and Health Department, it would have to be presented to the Minister and to the Department first before coming to the Committee. He felt that this would probably delay the presentation by at least one meeting.

Minibus up-grade

The third item on the agenda was the request by Evelyn Proudfoot for support for a general up-grade in the transport for the elderly. She reported that the current Minibuses were too small and were quite awkward for the elderly to enter. She said that some of the current vehicles were "for ever breaking down" which was not only costly but also meant that sometimes the elderly did not get to the Day Centres at all.

Janet asked for details of the number of breakdowns. She also asked why, on these occasions, another Regional Minibus had not been drafted in. Evelyn was unable to provide information on either of these points. Alec White stated that, if the larger Minibuses were purchased, it was likely that fewer of them would be required.

Hamish indicated that he felt it was not appropriate at this stage to make a decision on whether or not to support a general up-grade in the Minibuses. He suggested that the matter should be deferred until a future meeting after they had all had time to digest the report on the survey of the services provided by the Day Care Centres. They would then have a clearer picture of the transport needs of the elderly. He suggested that it would be helpful to the discussion at that meeting if Evelyn would produce a paper on the matter. He further suggested that, in the meantime, back-up cover from a neighbouring Minibus service should be requested in the event of a breakdown. These suggestions were agreed.

ACTION

You are asked to write the minutes for the above Ad Hoc Committee Meeting up to, and including, item 3 on the agenda.

Case 6.5
Effective minutes (3)

General objectives: To give further practice in the writing of minutes

Skills developed: Analysis
                            Decision-making
                            Minute-writing
                            Communication

BRITLAND HOME AND HEALTH DEPARTMENT (3)

Background

At the next meeting of the Ad Hoc Committee, held on 14 November at 2.30 pm in a Committee Room of the Britland offices, the regular Minute Clerk, John Clark, was present. So were the new members of the Committee agreed at the last Committee Meeting - James Wilson, Dr Irene Fisher and Alison Morris. Mrs Janet Clarkson had sent her apologies. (See Case 6.4 for details of the other members of the Committee.)

Ad Hoc Committee Meeting

Hamish Park opened the meeting by welcoming Mr Wilson, Dr Fisher and Mrs Morris. The minutes of the previous Ad Hoc Committee Meeting, which had been redrafted prior to circulation, were accepted. Hamish then proceeded to the "Matters arising".

The first item to be reported on was the matter of the increased membership of the Committee. Hamish reported that, as they would have already gathered, James Wilson and Irene Fisher had joined the Committee and that Alison Morris had gladly accepted the invitation to attend in a non-voting capacity.

The second item under "Matters arising" was the proposal, agreed at the previous meeting, to alternate the venues for future meetings between the BHHD offices and the Social Work Department. Hamish stated that it looked as if the proposal would have to be shelved at present because of structural repair work to the offices of the Social Work Department which was due to commence very shortly. Evelyn then pointed out that the major structural problem had only recently been discovered and that the repairs were likely to go on for a good number of months. She added that the repairs were going to present a major problem to the department as the departmental work was likely to be severely disrupted during this time.

James Wilson suggested that the Health Board would be only too pleased to supply accommodation for some meetings, provided the relevant premises were not already booked. Hamish asked James to investigate the availability of their premises for the next meeting and to let John Clark know the outcome as soon as possible.

Management of the Day Care Centre

The meeting then proceeded with the other items on the agenda. The first item, which had been requested by James Wilson, was the management of the Day Care Centres. Hamish asked James to speak to the item. James began by stating that he recognised that the Social Work Department, which currently managed the centres, did so with the best of intentions. He complimented the department on the enthusiasm of its staff but pointed out that, unfortunately, their enthusiasm was not matched by efficiency and that the management team lacked an appreciation of the real need for a much higher level of medical care.

At this point Evelyn, who was absolutely furious, interrupted James by loudly proclaiming that, since he had never run a Day Care Centre, he did not know what he was talking about. She forcibly drew his attention to the fact that any slight inefficiencies were caused by the poor accommodation and low-level facilities provided by the Regional Authorities and not by any lack of ability or efficiency in her staff. In this she was supported by Victor Hamilton. She continued by stating that she had always known that he was more interested in a "takeover" bid for the management of the Day Care Centres than in doing anything to improve the conditions for the old folks.

James responded by stating that Evelyn was talking absolute nonsense and that he had no *wish* to "take over" the service but recognised that this was probably the only solution if the elderly people who came to the centres were to get the attention they required. At this point, he asked Dr Fisher to outline her experiences of some of her elderly patients who had medical problems which should have been picked up by Day Care staff but appeared to have gone unnoticed. Dr Fisher did so, adding that, in her opinion, the problem could be solved if the Day Care Centres would combine social and health care by having a joint management team.

In an attempt to resolve the problem, Hamish asked Tom Dean to comment. He agreed with Dr Fisher and stated that he believed that equal involvement by the Social Work Department and the Health Board in the management of the Centres would be an excellent idea. Hamish then asked Alison for her opinion. She stated that she felt that this would only complicate matters but that she personally would not oppose the idea, particularly if it would resolve the current dispute. Evelyn pointed out that this would in fact only aggravate the situation.

Irene Fisher then stated that she would like to propose that each Day Care Centre should have a management team of three - one representative from the Social Work Department, one from the Health Board and one from the BHHD. She was seconded by Alec White. Hamish Park immediately intervened by stating that he did not think it was appropriate for a BHHD representative to be on the management team since the running of Day Care Centres was a local government and not a central government matter.

James Wilson agreed with Hamish and proposed an amendment that the management team of three should consist of two representatives from the Social Work Department and one from the Health Board. This was seconded by Victor Hamilton and carried by a majority of five to one.

Close of meeting

Hamish thanked the members for their attendance and reminded them that the next meeting would be on 28 November at the usual time and that they would be informed of the venue in the notice of the meeting.

ACTION

You are now asked to take the role of John Clark, the regular Minute Clerk of the Ad Hoc Committee, and draft the minutes for the Ad Hoc Committee Meeting.

Case 6.6
Meetings role-play

General objectives: To reinforce the trainee's understanding of the procedure of meetings

To develop skill in the running of a meeting and in the handling of contentious situations

To gain practical experience in minute-taking and subsequent minute-writing

Skills developed: Analysis
Decision-making
Chairing of a meeting
Verbal communication skills
Minute-taking
Minute-writing

MEETING 1

Notice of meeting and agenda

You are invited to attend a Management Meeting of Brook Transport Services PLC to be held in the Board Room on Friday 19 November 19.. at 1030 hours.

Agenda

1 Minutes of the meeting held on Friday 22 October 19.. (Paper A already circulated)

2 Matters arising - new category of haulage vehicle

3 Manpower reduction targets

4 New promotion campaign (Paper B)

5 Any other competent business

6 Date of next meeting: Friday 17 December 19.. at 1030 hours

Scenario

Over the last few years Brook Transport Services has experienced a number of problems with their administrative systems which have resulted in customer complaints and, in some cases, loss of orders. The general lack of efficiency has had an affect on costs which in turn has affected profitability.

To try to overcome these difficulties, the management is in the process of introducing a new computerised system to the administration. Initial discussions were held with the trade unions and assurances given that redundancies were very unlikely. Recent figures show, however, that the level of natural wastage (ie people leaving for one reason or another) is insufficient to meet the manpower reduction targets. There is serious concern that the company will require to consider making some people redundant.

The problems with the corporate image and also with fairly high charges to customers as a result of low efficiency and high costs, has led to a reduction in the company's market share. Over and above the planned introduction of a new computer system there is a proposal to hold a new promotion campaign.

Chairperson's brief

Welcome members to the meeting and ask if there are any apologies for absence.

Item 1 State that you are taking the minutes of the last meeting as having been read and ask the meeting if they can be accepted as being a correct record. (If there is general agreement round the meeting, you can merely note that the minutes have been accepted *or* you can ask for a proposer and seconder to accept the minutes. Both methods are used, although the former is probably more often adopted now.)

Item 2 As far as you are aware, there is only one matter arising. That is the proposal which was made at the last meeting to consider introducing a new category of haulage vehicle. Report to the meeting that an Ad Hoc Committee has been set up to investigate the situation. It held its first meeting two weeks ago and it is envisaged that there will be a report on its findings at the January Board Meeting.

Item 3 Ask the Personnel Officer to outline the current position as far as natural wastage is concerned and also to make recommendations which the meeting can discuss on how best to proceed to meet the required target figures.

Be prepared for some acrimony and heated discussion. Try to get agreement on the way forward. If necessary, take a vote on any

Item 4   Ask the Marketing Manager to talk to his paper which outlines his proposals for the new promotion campaign. When he has finished, invite the members to ask questions and then throw the issue open for discussion. Again try to get agreement on the course of action to be adopted, taking a vote if necessary.

Item 5   Deal as you wish with any item which arises. (I suspect that you may have little time for any matter under this item.)

Item 6   Close by thanking the members for their attendance and asking them to note the date and time of the next meeting.

Note:
Remember to watch your time. Make sure that you control the meeting. Do not let it "get out of hand". Do not let several people talk at once. Do not let one or two people monopolise the discussion (but be careful not to stifle discussion). Try to ensure that everyone who wants to speak to an item has the opportunity.

Minute Clerk's brief

Record who attends the meeting.

When the Chairperson asks for apologies, give the name of one of the members who has sent you apologies. Then note down any other apologies which are given.

Take notes of the meeting, fulfilling any other relevant duties which you are required to undertake. After the meeting write up the minutes.

ACTION

You are asked to prepare for the meeting by reading over the notice, agenda, scenario and your brief. You should then hold the prescribed meeting, adopting the role which has been given to you in your brief.

MEETING 2

Notice of meeting and agenda

The next meeting of the Directors of the Thistle Leisure Centres will be held in the Meeting Room on Wednesday 12 May 19.. at 1630 hours.

Agenda

1 Minutes of the last meeting held on Wednesday 10 March 19.. (Paper A already circulated)

2 Matters arising - Craiglee Director

3 Equal opportunities policy

4 Increase in subscriptions (Paper B)

5 Proposed new leisure centre

6 Date of next meeting: Wednesday 30 June 19.. at 1630 hours

Scenario

Thistle Leisure Centres is an organisation providing leisure facilities in a number of towns and cities. Each centre is run by a full-time Director and a small number of staff. Expertise in a number of areas (eg finance, personnel, marketing) is provided from Head Office which is attached to one of the largest leisure centres. Members of the centres pay a fee on first joining and thereafter an annual subscription which allows them access to the full range of facilities in the centre.

There has been considerable expansion over the last few years both in membership and in the number of centres. This has led to quite a few new posts, a number of which have been filled by means of internal promotions.

In connection with the recent recruitment drive, there have been two complaints from female members of staff about lack of equal opportunities. In both instances the complainants were not interviewed for a vacancy. They have claimed sexual discrimination because the interviewees were all male with shorter periods of service and were, in their opinion, less well qualified. Although it is not the remit of the meeting to discuss the individual cases or the reasons why the two female members of staff were not interviewed, there is general concern that the company policy of equal opportunity has been called into question. The meeting is being asked to discuss what measures should be taken to improve the company image and to avoid any likelihood of legal action, which one complainant is currently threatening to take.

There has been a proposal from the Finance Director to raise the subscription level, which he feels is ridiculously low.

Chairperson's brief

Welcome members to the meeting and ask if there are any apologies for absence.

Item 1   State that you are taking the minutes of the last meeting as "having been read" and ask the meeting if they can be accepted as being a correct record. (If there is general agreement round the meeting, you can merely note that the minutes have been accepted *or* you can ask for a proposer and seconder to accept the minutes. Both methods are used although the former is probably more often adopted now.)

Item 2   As far as you are aware, there is only one matter arising - the vacancy for a Director for the Craiglee Leisure Centre. Report to the meeting that, as will have been noticed, the post was advertised a few weeks ago and interviews will be held shortly. Indicate that there has been considerable interest in the post and that you hope for a successful outcome.

Item 3   Ask the Personnel Officer to outline the current position regarding the organisation's policy on equal opportunities. Thereafter, throw the meeting open for discussion on how best to improve the company's image in the minds of staff, which will prevent a similar situation occurring in future.

Be prepared for some acrimony and heated discussion. Try to get agreement on the way forward. If necessary, take a vote on any proposals and amendments, remembering to note the names of the proposers and seconders.

Item 4   Ask the Finance Director to talk to his paper which outlines his proposals for increased subscriptions. Thereafter, invite the members to ask questions and then throw the issue open for discussion. Again try to get agreement on the course of action to be adopted, taking a vote if necessary.

Item 5   Deal with this item as you wish. (I suspect that you may have little time for it.)

Item 6   Close by thanking the members for their attendance and asking them to note the date and time of the next meeting.

(See note at the end of the Chairperson's brief in meeting 1 on page 93.)

Minute Clerk's brief

(See relevant notes in meeting 1 on page 93.)

ACTION

You are asked to prepare for the meeting by reading over the notice, agenda, scenario and your brief. You should then hold the prescribed meeting, adopting the role which has been given to you in your brief.

MEETING 3

Notice of meeting and agenda

The next meeting of the Industrial Relations Committee of the Horton Hills Hotel will be held in the Conference Suite on Tuesday 16 February 19.. at 1030 hours.

Agenda

1. Minutes of the last meeting held on Tuesday 19 January 19.. (Paper A already circulated)

2. Matters arising - job evaluation scheme

3. New staff hours (Paper B)

4. The AIDS issue

5. Proposed new chalets

6. Date of next meeting: Tuesday 16 March 19.. at 1030 hours

Scenario

The Horton Hills Hotel - a very large hotel set in extensive grounds - incorporates a number of leisure facilities as well as the main hotel. Once a month there is a meeting between the hotel management and the various trade union representatives.

In order to improve efficiency, the Personnel Manager and the Finance Director are proposing to change staff hours. There will be no change to the overall number of hours worked but there will be changes to the shift times for all staff. The trade union representatives have already indicated their concern at the changes, which they think will result in a deterioration in staff conditions. They are particularly concerned about the proposed hours for the dining room staff. There have always been split shifts but, in their opinion, the proposal will worsen the situation. The management view is that, on a number of shifts, the dining room staff will now have more time off in the middle of the day and the system will increase the productivity of the hotel.

The second issue to be discussed at this meeting is that one of the kitchen staff has recently been found to be HIV positive. There is already considerable concern among the other staff. The management and trade union representatives feel it is vital that they deal with this current problem and also establish a general policy on AIDS.

Chairperson's brief

Welcome members to the meeting and ask if there are any apologies for absence.

Item 1   State that you are taking the minutes of the last meeting as having been read and ask the meeting if they can be accepted as being a correct record. (If there is general agreement round the meeting, you can merely note that the minutes have been accepted *or* you can ask for a proposer and seconder to accept the minutes. Both methods are used although the former is probably more often adopted now.)

Item 2   As far as you are aware, there is only one matter arising - the proposed new job evaluation scheme. At the last meeting it was decided to investigate the implementation of a new job evaluation scheme. Report to the meeting that an Ad Hoc Committee has been established with a remit to investigate the situation and make recommendations on the structure of the new scheme. It has already met twice and will be reporting to the next meeting.

Item 3   Ask the Personnel Officer to outline the proposal for the new staff hours. Thereafter, throw the meeting open for discussion.

Be prepared for some acrimony and heated discussion. Try to get agreement on the way forward. If necessary, take a vote on any proposals and amendments, remembering to note the names of the proposers and seconders.

Item 4   Ask the senior trade union official to start the discussion and outline any proposals he/she would like to put to the meeting. Thereafter, throw the issue open for discussion. Again try to get agreement on the course of action to be adopted, taking a vote if necessary.

Item 5 Deal with this item as you wish. (I suspect that you may have little time for it.)

Item 6 Close by thanking the members for their attendance and asking them to note the date and time of the next meeting.

(See note at the end of the Chairperson's brief in meeting 1 on page 93.)

Minute Clerk's brief

(See relevant notes in meeting 1 on page 93.)

ACTION

You are asked to prepare for the meeting by reading over the notice, agenda, scenario and your brief. You should then hold the prescribed meeting, adopting the role which has been given to you in your brief.

Notes to Tutor

The number of members attending the meetings is not given. It is useful to have a reasonable number of students in any one meeting - seven or eight would be best.

As well as being given the notice of meeting, the agenda and the scenario, each student should be given a brief. Briefs are given for the Chairperson and the Minute Clerk, and similar ones should be written for the others.

The length of briefs may vary. Some may be very short; others should be specific as to how the student should react to one or more items on the agenda. When designing the briefs it is important to ensure that someone is given the role of the Manager who has presented a paper or who has been designated to talk on an issue. Make sure that a student is given notice that he/she will be asked to talk to a paper or to a particular issue. Built into the role descriptors should be some element of contention. It is also a good idea to give some freedom to the students on how to react to certain issues, although they should always react in keeping with the character assigned to them. Examples of the type of information which can be given in the brief are as follows.

General

a You are well known as a "peace-maker" who tries to get people to accept compromise and also tries to prevent arguments. Be prepared for trouble in item 4. Otherwise react as you want as long as it is in character with the role descriptor.

b You do not "get on" with the Personnel Officer [or whoever] and cannot hide your feelings. React as you wish on other items.

c You are a bit of a "moaner" and tend to be against change in principle. Argue from this stance.

Meeting 1

a Be prepared to support the idea that the organisation tried its best to accommodate the unions but now has no alternative but to introduce redundancies. In your opinion the unions will just have to accept this.

b Make the point that you consider that the organisation is committed to avoiding redundancies. Suggest an offer of early retirement for staff.

c Support the idea of voluntary redundancies and propose that you offer very generous terms.

Meeting 2

a You support the Personnel Officer and feel that little more can be done to prevent the complaint arising again.

b You are the Manager of the department in which the complainants work. Although the remit of the meeting does not extend to discussing the details of the cases of either complainant, you are determined to do so. *Immediately* the Chairperson pauses for breath after having introduced item 3, launch a very strong verbal attack on the Personnel Officer whom you consider to have caused the whole problem.

c Be prepared to make a report on the suggested increase in the subscriptions. Point out that, although the leisure centres are very popular and have large memberships, the income from subscriptions is low. Argue that, given the wide range of facilities available, an increase in subscriptions would be more than justified and would merely bring the subscriptions into line with other similar bodies.

Meeting 3

a Be prepared to talk to the issue. You feel very strongly that a change in hours is required if the profitability of the organisation is to be maintained in the future.

b Argue strongly against the new hours. Give two reasons for this strong stance and be prepared to defend your stance "to the death"!

c You feel very strongly that no action should be taken against the member who is HIV positive. You forcibly point out that he poses no threat to the public or to the other staff. Be prepared to defend your point of view vigorously.

d You feel that little needs to be done since the virus cannot be passed on through food. You feel that, provided the member of staff agrees to take appropriate precautions, there is no danger to other staff or to guests.

e You feel that the employee should not be made to suffer as a result of his being HIV positive and are therefore ready to fight against any attempt to dismiss him. You are also concerned, however, about your other members, many of whom have already spoken to you about fears of being infected since the employee handles knives and other implements which might result in him cutting himself.

f Although you feel sorry for the member of staff concerned, it is your opinion that he cannot carry on in his current post because of the likely public reaction if the situation became known. Suggest that he is transferred to the vacant post of Assistant Groundsman.

SECTION 7
THE INDIVIDUAL WITHIN THE ORGANISATION

Most organisations have a Personnel Department, two of the responsibilities of which are manpower planning and recruitment. Although the specialist expertise in these areas will lie with staff in the Personnel Department, it is vital for administrative and management staff in other departments to have an understanding of the problems and techniques associated with manpower planning and recruitment since they will have to play an important part in both of these areas. This section examines three aspects - the principles and procedures of manpower planning, recruitment and selection interviewing.

As far as manpower planning is concerned, all Managers must understand the principles and practice since they are responsible for the functioning of their department, which will be neither efficient nor effective if it does not have the right staff with the right skills. The only way to ensure that a department has sufficient, appropriately-trained staff, at any given time, is to undertake manpower planning in advance of that time.

It is normal for a Manager to be party to the recruitment process. This is most likely to include the drawing up or re-assessment of job descriptions and personnel specifications (job specifications). The following case therefore gives the student practice in drawing up both these documents and in identifying methods of attracting and selecting suitable applicants.

Selection interviewing is a skill which will be required of many administrators and managers. Poor technique is likely either to result in selecting the wrong person or in losing the best person. An understanding of the technique will go some way to help the individual in developing effective interview skills.

Case 7.1
Manpower planning

General objectives: To reinforce learning on manpower planning

To relate theories on manpower planning to a practical situation

To analyse the case and make recommendations

Skills developed: Analysis
Problem-solving
Decision-making

RAWLINGS MANUFACTURING PLC

Background

Rawlings Manufacturing is a medium-sized manufacturing company situated on the outskirts of a large industrial town. Traditionally, the company has had a fairly high rate of labour turnover, partly because of the relatively unskilled nature of much of the work and also because of the number of organisations competing in the same job market. The labour turnover among the office staff has tended to be lower than that of the production workers.

Each year Rawlings has targeted school-leavers for both manufacturing and office staff. It has always been organisational policy to send office staff under the age of 18 on day-release to the local college to increase their skills and qualifications. Most of the office staff received their training in this way and have been with the company for many years.

Increasing computerisation

As with many similar companies, Rawlings has been increasing the amount of computerisation in their administration. Most of the clerical staff use a computer terminal for at least part of their day and many for much longer. It must be said, however, that their knowledge of the computer is limited to the use of the software package relevant to their particular job. The training for this was carried out in-house and consisted of one or two days of hands-on training. Secretarial staff, who traditionally used only a typewriter, have also had to undergo an in-house training course - in their case for word processing.

Future manpower planning

Two years ago Rawlings decided to undertake a major assessment of future manpower needs and the Personnel Department was asked to investigate the situation regarding current staffing. Using the Personnel records, they drew up a report which gave a breakdown of the age of all staff, their qualifications, the department in which they worked and the in-house training they had received. The report also contained a breakdown of the average qualifications, etc, of the school-leavers they recruited, as it was anticipated that the company would continue to employ approximately the same number of school-leavers each year.

Representatives from the Personnel Department then held a meeting with Department Managers to ascertain the skills which they envisaged staff would require over the next five years. Using the two sets of information, the Personnel Department drew up a training programme to equip their staff with the skills needed for the foreseeable future.

Two years on

There was deep concern, two years on, to discover that the situation was not as good as the company had anticipated. Eighteen months previously, another company, which had been negotiating for over a year to take over an empty factory and office block, at last "clinched" the deal. They opened nine months later. Prior to this time they had carried out a major recruitment drive. Since their wages were higher than the average and the skills they required were, in many cases, similar to those of Rawlings, the labour turnover at Rawlings increased dramatically.

Rawlings found that they were unable to make up for the shortfall by employing more school-leavers, as the numbers applying for vacancies also dropped drastically. The management was very concerned and initially blamed the newly-opened company for the problems. Further enquiries, however, highlighted the fact that they had not recruited as many school-leavers as in the past, preferring to recruit ready-trained staff.

A review of the performance of the remaining staff at Rawlings was also rather disappointing. The level of IT knowledge had certainly increased but more slowly than anticipated, and a number of staff had appeared either to be very reluctant to adopt the new techniques or had expressed lack of confidence and fears about using their new skills. The problem was compounded by a decrease in the rate of planned training which had occurred during the same period. This had been forced on Rawlings as a result of a fall in profits caused by the continuing recession and also because of the delay in solving a production problem which had haunted them for almost 18 months. The problem had finally been overcome only about a year ago.

In addition, requests were only now being received from some of the Managers for staff with a greater base of theoretical knowledge and considerable analytical and problem-solving ability. Two of the Managers suggested that they should be looking to the local Polytechnic/University to recruit some of its recent graduates.

ACTION

1 Read the case and identify any evidence of good practice in manpower planning by Rawlings Manufacturing plc.

2 Identify the problems being experienced by Rawlings.

3 From your knowledge of manpower planning, do you consider that any of these problems have been caused by poor manpower planning on the part of Rawlings? If so, examine the areas of manpower planning where the problems have occurred.

4 What action would you recommend Rawlings should take to overcome its problems?

Case 7.2
Recruitment

General objectives: To reinforce learning on the factors to be considered when recruiting staff

To relate theoretical knowledge on recruitment to a practical situation

To differentiate between a job description and a personnel specification (job specification)

To draw up a job description and a personnel specification (job specification)

Skills developed: Analysis
Decision-making
Drafting a job description and a personnel specification (job specification)

JAMES HANLEY PLC

Background

James Hanley plc is a medium-sized engineering company situated in a large industrial estate in the north-east of England. Its business has expanded greatly over the past two years, particularly in the export market, although home sales have also increased. The net result has been that the company has doubled its workforce - mainly on the engineering side although one or two administrative staff have also been recruited. The general office is divided into several sections, one of which handles all the document production for the company, except for that of the Managing Director who has his own Personal Secretary.

Introduction of office information system

Within the last year there have been a lot of changes in the office - the principal one being the introduction of a sophisticated office information system. Prior to that time the company had a small computer which was used by the Finance Department and documents were produced on word processing equipment.

Because of the greater demands placed on administration by the organisational expansion and the desire to gain some of the benefits which could come from increased use of information technology, it was decided to purchase a new, integrated information system. At the same time, it was decided that efficiency would be improved by restructuring the office organisation and introducing a system of flexitime for all staff.

Staffing the Document Production Centre

The Typing Supervisor, who is a very capable lady with a number of years' experience in the company, was promoted to the post of Document Production Manager in charge of the entire Document Production Centre. This was divided into two sections and consisted of nine staff in total. The larger of the two sections was to handle all the general document requirements of the company. The smaller section (consisting of a total of three members of staff) would deal with the overseas correspondence and documentation, most of which was with South American countries and much of which was in Spanish. It was decided that the Senior Typist would become the Supervisor of the General Section and that the organisation should recruit a Supervisor for the Overseas Section.

In order to attract someone with the right skills and experience, it was decided to offer an annual salary of £10 000. The organisation also took the decision that the Supervisors would be responsible for training within their sections. In addition, it was expected that they would liaise with the Document Production Manager, with the Managers of the various specialist departments and with the Computer Manager to develop systems which would use the equipment to its maximum efficiency.

ACTION

1 From your own experience and using the information given in the case, construct a job description for the post of Overseas Supervisor in the Document Production Centre within James Hanley plc.

2 Using the job description, now draw up a personnel specification (job specification) for the Overseas Supervisor.

3 Given that the job description and personnel specification have been drawn up, how would you set about attracting suitable applicants?

4 What methods of selection would you consider to be most appropriate for the Overseas Supervisor? Who would you suggest should take part in the selection process?

Case 7.3
Selection interviewing

General objectives: To reinforce learning on interviewing techniques

To relate theoretical learning to a practical situation

To analyse the case

To make a presentation on the skill of selection interviewing

To compare selection interviewing techniques with techniques for other kinds of interviews

Skills developed: Analysis
Problem-solving
Decision-making
Verbal communication
Presentation skills

KIRSTEN MACLEAN

Background

My name is Kirsten MacLean and I am currently a Manager of the administrative function in a large legal practice. Since leaving college eight years ago with a Higher National Diploma in Secretarial Studies, I have worked with three different organisations. My first two jobs were secretarial posts in which I gained fairly wide experience. My third job was with my current employer - initially as a Personal Secretary and latterly as Manager of the administrative function for the entire legal practice. In this role I have to manage a number of secretarial/clerical staff, a range of equipment and a wide variety of different systems, both manual and computerised.

Over a number of years I have been studying for an Open University degree, which I am happy to say I obtained at the end of last year. One of my principal aims in studying for the degree was to gain sufficient qualifications to enter a teaching career. In the past three years I have taught an evening class one night a week in order to gain some teaching experience. To further my teaching ambitions, I recently applied for three lecturing posts in local colleges and was fortunate to be called for interview by two of the colleges. The following are descriptions of my two interview experiences.

College Alpha

I received a letter calling me for interview two weeks before the date. The letter contained particulars of where to go and whom to ask for. When I arrived at the college I made my way to the second floor and to the room number I had been given. I was rather daunted to receive no reply to my knock on the door. Fortunately a Lecturer who was passing asked if he could help me. He guided me to a room two doors along, explaining that the rooms had been renumbered recently and the door on which I had been knocking was now a cupboard!

During the course of the morning I and the other candidates met the Head of Department and the Senior Lecturers and were shown round the department. My interview was in the early afternoon and I was second to be called. There were four members on the panel seated at one side of a fairly large table - the Assistant Principal, the Head of Department, one of the Senior Lecturers and a member of the administrative staff.

College Alpha interview

The Assistant Principal welcomed me to the college and invited me to take a seat at the other side of the table. He opened the questioning by asking me why I had applied for the job and what skill I thought I could bring to the department. He continued by asking me to expand on my statements on the application form about my qualifications and experience both in business and in teaching. The Head of Department was then invited to ask some questions. She asked me for my opinion on some of the trends in business education and where I thought developments would come in the future.

The Senior Lecturer followed by commenting that, in his experience, staff were expected to undertake quite a lot of work outside normal working hours and asked if I would be willing to spend a fair amount of evening time either at home or at college in preparing for my classes. He next asked me how many hours a week I would expect to spend working at home in the evening and whether or not I had family commitments which would make this difficult. His final questions were about how I would discipline a class which was causing problems.

The Assistant Principal then asked the member of administrative staff to talk about salary and conditions and, just before the end of the interview, asked me if I had any questions. He indicated that they had all the information they needed and thanked me for attending the interview. The interview had lasted about half an hour. I made my way back to the waiting room and found the first candidate still there. He did not seem to know whether or not he was expected to go or stay. I stated that since no-one had said one thing or the other, I was going home.

College Beta

Notification for the second interview came four days before the interview date. It could not have come at a worse time because there were one or two urgent jobs which had to be completed and everyone was already working late on them. Because of this I had to work on the morning of my interview and was slightly later leaving than I had intended. As a result I had a rush to get to the college on time and had some difficulty in finding the right building. After asking my way from two members of the general public, I found the college but was horrified to discover how busy the car park was. Further investigation showed that it was completely full and that there were several notices warning against parking on yellow lines and hatched areas. I tried the streets round about with no immediate success. Eventually I managed to get a space in the college car park when someone left.

By the time I found my way into the building, which was no easy task, I realised that I was five minutes late. In some agitation I made my way to the general office, as the Janitor's office was empty. After knocking on the window twice, a girl came and asked if she could help me. I indicated that I was here for an interview and asked where I should go. The girl looked blankly at me and said that she would try to find out. About five minutes later, when she had not re-appeared, I again knocked at the window. This time an older woman came. I repeated my story and she also undertook to try to find out where I was to go. She came back fairly quickly and directed me to a room on the third floor.

When I got there I found two people waiting. I asked what was happening and they indicated that nothing had happened so far, other than the Departmental Secretary coming into the room and stating that she was sorry the interviews would be a little delayed. I was glad when she came in again and took a note of my presence. She gave me the same story about the delay and left the room. Three-quarters of an hour later, after we had just about given up hope, she reappeared and invited me to come along. I left the others in the room and followed her.

College Beta interview

There were only two members on the panel and no-one from the administration. The Principal apologised for the delay and stated that he and the Head of Department had been at a Board Meeting which had lasted longer than expected. He asked me a number of direct questions about my qualifications and experience. I must admit to being a bit irritated by some of the questions which I felt I had answered clearly in the application form. He then asked me what particular subjects I would like to teach. When I indicated my preference he passed me over to the Head of Department who spent some time telling me about the department, the subject areas taught and the job for which I had applied. He again asked me what subject area I would like to teach! I found it quite difficult to keep the annoyance out of my voice as I answered him. Before handing the questioning back to the Principal, he said that it would appear from what I had said about my experience that I had quite a considerable knowledge of different IT software packages. When I answered in the affirmative, he asked me to go into some detail about one of them.

The Principal then asked why I was interested in teaching and enquired about my personal interests and commitments. He gave me some particulars about the conditions of the job and said that, if I were offered the job, details of the salary would be included with the offer letter. He finished by asking me if I had any questions and, after replying to my questions, thanked me for coming. He added that they had still to interview more candidates and stated that I would be notified of the result of the interview - probably in about two weeks' time.

ACTION

1 Read the case and examine any instances of poor practice and/or techniques in the arranging and conducting of the two interviews.

2 Comment on any evidence you have identified of good practice and/or techniques in relation to the interviews.

3 What types of question technique were used in the course of the two interviews? Comment on the appropriateness and the value of the question techniques used in the case.

4 Using the information gleaned from the case, along with your wider knowledge of interview techniques, prepare a presentation on the skill of selection interviewing which you might give at a Management Development Training course.

5 What points discussed in this case would be relevant to the conduct of an appraisal interview? What other factors should be considered?

6 What points discussed in this case would be relevant to the conduct of a disciplinary interview? What other factors should be considered?

SECTION 8
MANAGING CHANGE

One thing which all organisations must face today is change. Greater changes in working life and practice have occurred in the last few years than in the whole of the rest of the century. One of the principle causes of change in the business world is the continued development of computerisation, and information technology in particular. Many organisations have made every endeavour to ensure that they have the most appropriate equipment and systems to maximise their potential. They have, however, paid little attention to the other vital area of the management of change - the human relations aspect.

People are central to the effective management of change and it is vital to understand their attitudes and potential reaction to change if the process is to be implemented successfully. Since their attitudes and reactions will be coloured by their perception of the effects that the change(s) will have on them, considerable attention must be given to ensuring that these effects are positive, not only for the organisation but also for the individual.

This section therefore examines a number of the areas which will be affected by the process of change and especially change related to information technology. These areas include training, job design, job evaluation and ergonomics, health and safety. The section also examines the change planning process itself, the causes of resistance to change and methods for preventing or overcoming resistance to change. It finally gives practice in the development of negotiation skills, which are vital for individuals or groups who wish to play a full part in the change process and to be able to negotiate terms and conditions which are, at the very least, acceptable to them.

Case 8.1
Planning change

General objectives: To reinforce understanding of the theories of planning change

To develop ability to relate the theoretical principles of planning for change to a practical situation

Skills developed: Analysis
Decision-making

BROWN & WILSON PLC (1)

Background

Brown and Wilson plc is an expanding organisation sited in a city centre. The organisation was established in the early 1950s as a wholesaler of ladies' fashions in the medium-priced bracket and quickly built up a clientele of small shops around the city and in towns in nearby districts. Problems first occurred in the late 1960s and early 1970s when the organisation was faced with severe competition from the far eastern countries. At first management had not been fully aware of what was happening. When the situation became clear, however, they decided that something must be done. In response to the problem the organisation diversified into children's clothing, which they felt was an area sufficiently closely allied to ladies' fashions to allow them to use their existing staff expertise.

The move brought considerable improvement in the situation in the short-term but did not provide a long-term solution, as some of Brown & Wilson's competitors took similar action, while organisations in other areas of the market tried to increase their sales by moving into ladies' fashions. A number of Brown & Wilson's suppliers, also facing severe competition, were either forced out of business altogether or were involved in mergers with other suppliers. The situation was further complicated by the fact that a few of their suppliers started direct selling to large chain stores which made it difficult for Brown & Wilson to obtain a sufficient range of goods at the price level which their customers wanted.

New marketing plan

Faced with a situation of threatened bankruptcy, the Directors realised that drastic action was required. Joe Cairns, who was a fairly new Director in the organisation, suggested that the solution was to change the whole market strategy. He proposed that the organisation should pull out of the highly competitive, medium-priced market and concentrate on the "top end" of the market. He also suggested that the range of goods supplied should be cut, which would enable the organisation to reduce losses by concentrating on supplying a fairly limited range of exclusive garments. In addition, he strongly advocated that the organisation, while still retaining the wholesale side of the business, should move increasingly into the retail end of the market.

Reactions to the new strategy

This radical plan met with considerable opposition from some of the older Directors who felt that the risk the company was being asked to take was far too great. Joe, however, managed to gain support from sufficient members of the Board to enable further investigation to be carried out. This investigation took the form of a market survey conducted by a team of independent researchers. When their report was published it indicated that there was considerable merit in the ideas which Joe had first suggested. The Board Meeting to discuss the findings of the report was a very stormy one. With a few minor amendments, however, the recommendations of the researchers were adopted by a fairly narrow majority. Three of the older Directors, who had consistently opposed the proposed changes and who had voted against the adoption of the report's recommendations, resigned a short time after the meeting.

This change was closely followed by others in the management of the organisation - one of the first of which was the early retirement of the Marketing Manager and the appointment of a new Manager. In line with the new policy, he began by actively seeking new manufacturers who designed eye-catching clothes for children and fashion-conscious women in their twenties and thirties. He obtained a particularly good supplier of matching "mother and child" outfits, which subsequently proved to be very popular and were the start of a new line for the organisation.

The first half of the 1980s was one of continued development for the organisation. The principal changes were the decline in the wholesale end of the market and a major face-lift for the organisation's premises to make them more attractive to the general public. During this time also, the organisation began an active advertising campaign in selected high-quality newspapers and magazines. The result was a much higher profile for the organisation and a marked increase in its turnover.

Mail order service

During the recession in the late 1980s it became clear that the organisation was going through a difficult period. Growth stopped and turnover began to fall slightly. This period also saw the retirement of the Managing Director. He was replaced by a younger, ambitious Director who, in the early 1980s, had been the first female Director of the company. She gained much local publicity on her appointment and determined to make her mark on the organisation.

Her first move was to propose that the organisation should extend and develop its informal mail order service with catalogues being distributed four times a year. She reported that this had been a very successful marketing strategy adopted by an organisation for which she had previously worked. This, she suggested, would not only increase turnover but would also widen the customer base. The Board, after considerable discussion, agreed to market research being undertaken. As on the previous occasion, the research report was favourable. The Directors, while recognising that the venture would have a high initial cost, agreed to establish a mail order service and the Managing Director was given authority to undertake what steps were necessary to set up the service.

ACTION

1 Read the case and identify any examples of good or bad planning practice on the part of Brown & Wilson plc.

2 What principles of good or bad planning do they exemplify?

Case 8.2
Planning and managing change

General objectives: To reinforce understanding of the theories of planning change

To develop ability to relate the theories of planning and managing change to a practical situation

To analyse the case and make recommendations

To produce a set of guidelines on planning for change

Skills developed: Analysis
Problem-solving
Decision-making
Documenting procedures
Communication skills

BROWN & WILSON PLC (2)

Background

As described in Case 8.1, Brown and Wilson plc is an expanding organisation sited in a city centre. The organisation was established in the early 1950s as a wholesaler of ladies' fashions in the medium-priced bracket. During the 1970s the organisation underwent a period of major change when it first of all diversified into children's clothing and subsequently concentrated on a fairly limited range of exclusive and more expensive garments. The organisation also developed into the retail sector as the wholesale side of the business declined.

Further problems in the late 1980s led to a proposal by the new Managing Director to move into the mail order business. She was given authority by the Board of Directors to undertake what steps were necessary to introduce the new mail order service.

New computer system

The Managing Director set up a project team consisting of the Marketing Manager, the Finance Director, the Computing Manager and the Personnel Manager to plan and oversee the implementation of the new service. Early in their discussions it became clear that an upgrade of the computer was required. This was reported to the subsequent Management Meeting and approval was given for the upgrade.

The project team then started work on the plans for any necessary redeployment and retraining of staff. At this point they initiated discussions with Managers of Departments which would be affected by the proposed changes and, in particular, with those where there would be redeployment of staff. Discussions were also held with trade union officials, who were given assurances that there would be no job losses as a result of the changes. When the trade union officials indicated concern over the changes in job content, the Personnel Manager pointed out that, had it not been for this new development, the management would probably at this time have been coming to discuss job cuts with the unions. The trade union officials rather reluctantly agreed to support the new developments, provided that full discussions were held with the members whose jobs would change significantly and any necessary training was given. There was also agreement that, after the initial implementation period was over, a job re-evaluation would be carried out for any jobs where there had been major changes.

Implementation of the changes

The project team complimented itself when it achieved the computer upgrade and the launch of the new service within four months of the Board decision and in time to catch the winter and pre-Christmas shopping market. The team felt that the level of interest displayed by the public justified their decision to move into the mail order business and also the considerable cost of marketing the new service. They were confident that the capital cost of the venture would be recouped well within the target period.

It soon became evident that the initial optimism of the project team was premature. Orders continued to exceed the targets set by management before the launch but a significant number of problems began to arise. The problems resulted in a barrage of customer complaints - considerably more than would normally have been expected even with the launch of such a major new project.

Management investigation

A management investigation of the situation highlighted the following points:

1 Many of the complaints stated that the goods were not received within the stated delivery period. Investigation showed that a significant number of goods ordered for Christmas had not been despatched until the second week of

January. Although the number of orders certainly exceeded expectations, the increase was not such as to account for the length of the delays.

2   Some of the delays resulted from errors and omissions by customers when completing the order form. Such orders were passed to one section for following up and a backlog of work had built up there.

3   The investigations also revealed that a number of orders which had been received seemed subsequently to have got lost in the processing.

4   There had also been a number of telephone calls from customers wishing to place orders by telephone. Although a section had been set up to deal with such telephone calls, customer complaints were received about the slowness of staff in dealing with the calls, particularly when the customer wished to query anything.

5   A number of the staff taking the telephone calls had been very upset by some of the customers as they felt that they were being blamed for problems which were not of their making. The Personnel Manager had received quite a few requests from such staff for transfer to another section as they did not have the skill to cope with the stress of dealing with telephone orders and the problems which arose.

6   There was a lot of general grumbling among staff about loss of job satisfaction. A number of the staff also stated that they had known that there would be problems as soon as they had been told the details of the new system. It appeared that some of the problems had been in existence before but were being highlighted and aggravated by the demands of the new system. The project team indicated that they had been unaware of the existence of such problems.

7   Investigation in one section where there were particular problems brought to light the fact that some of the staff were not too clear about the new procedures and what was being demanded of them.

8   The Personnel Manager indicated that the staff turnover in the last three months had been higher than usual. This was causing major difficulties for certain sections which were understaffed. The loss of trained staff, the additional pressure on remaining staff and the inexperience of new staff were resulting in increased errors in these sections.

The Managing Director was very concerned about the problems. In reading through one of her management journals she came across an article which looked at the success story of a mail order company. The article highlighted the extent to which the success of the company was linked to the sophisticated integrated information system which they had installed. The Managing Director discussed the article with the Computer Manager and both agreed that such a system could greatly improve the situation in Brown & Wilson.

ACTION

1. Analyse the case of Brown & Wilson plc (2) and identify any problems which are being experienced.

2. Examine the causes of the problems and identify where any of them could be the result of bad practice in the planning for change.

3. In your analysis of the case, did you identify any instances of good practice in the planning of change? What principles do these good practices exemplify?

4. What recommendations would you make to Brown & Wilson to overcome their current problems?

5. Prepare a set of guidelines which an organisation could follow when planning and managing change.

Case 8.3
Overcoming resistance to change

General objectives: To identify causes of resistance to change

To identify policies to prevent or overcome resistance to change

To analyse the case and make recommendations

Skills developed: Analysis
Problem-solving
Decision-making
Report-writing
Communication

HAMILTON SUPPLIES PLC

Background

Hamilton Supplies plc is a large wholesale office supplies organisation with customers all over the country. The organisation is sited in a warehouse near a city centre and has a large number of office staff, mainly women, involved in clerical and secretarial work. A high percentage of the female employees are married with families.

The organisation has recently been facing severe competition and the management has recognised that, if they are to retain their share of the market, they will have to make substantial changes to their marketing strategy and administrative procedures.

Hiring of Consultants

Two months ago the management hired a firm of Consultants to examine the issue and make recommendations. In an attempt to scotch rumours and minimise uncertainty, management recently informed the workforce of the serious problem which the company was facing and of the work being done by the Consultants to investigate the situation and suggest ways in which the position could be remedied. At the same time management issued a statement that they hoped to be able to retain all the staff but that, if this were not possible, they would offer generous redundancy terms.

The Consultants' report

The report produced by the Consultants recommended that the organisation should change from mainly manual procedures to a sophisticated integrated computer system which would link the distribution, clerical and secretarial work. To do this effectively they recommended that the organisation move to a greenfield site on the northern outskirts of the city and take over a large unit in a new industrial estate which was due for completion in a month's time. They recommended that the organisational structure be examined with a view to streamlining it by combining departments.

They pointed out that the new system would involve the organisation in scrapping their existing and fairly limited computer equipment as well as their electronic typewriters and current word processing equipment. All staff, from the management downwards, would be required to learn to operate the new system. They recommended that the secretarial staff should be trained in the use of spreadsheet and desktop publishing software as well as text processing software.

Reaction to the report and subsequent management action

The General Manager was enthusiastic about the report's recommendations, as he felt that this would improve the company's market position, would result in jobs becoming much more interesting and challenging for staff, and would provide more spacious and pleasant premises in which to work.

The report received a very mixed reception when it was discussed at the next Management Meeting. A number of the Managers expressed serious reservations over whether or not such drastic changes were required. Some indicated that they could foresee no occasion when they themselves would require to use the technology since all that kind of work would be undertaken by their clerical and secretarial staff. Two of them also indicated that they had found the current computer system to be of limited use to their departments because a lot of work still required to be done manually and the Data Processing Manager did not seem interested in, or capable of meeting their departmental needs. Despite this, however, the General Manager succeeded in getting a narrow majority in favour of implementing the report.

As a first stage, the General Manager called in the Data Processing Manager, who was very enthusiastic about the project, and asked him to take charge of the operation. The General Manager asked the Data Processing Manager to contact the computer supplier and arrange for the installation of the system and to liaise with the Personnel Manager over necessary training.

The General Manager called a meeting of all the staff to inform them of the report's recommendations and the management decision to implement these in full. He was very surprised at the hostile reaction which the staff displayed at the meeting and was angry that a number of the Departmental Managers sat silent throughout the meeting and did not support him. He was subsequently furious when, the next day, he received a deputation from the APEX shop stewards representing clerical and secretarial staff, stating that their members were strongly opposed to the proposals which had come as a great surprise to them. The shop stewards threatened industrial action.

ACTION

1 Analyse the case study and identify reasons for the hostile attitude among the various staff groups.

2 How could such a reaction have been avoided?

3 You are an independent Consultant from a nearby Polytechnic who has been brought in to Hamilton Supplies. Given the *current situation* in the company, as described in the case, write a report to the General Manager which recommends what course of action the management could *now* take to overcome the various problems.

Case 8.4
Training

General objectives: To identify and analyse some of the issues which can arise when designing a training programme

To gain an understanding of some of the factors involved in the design of an IT training programme

To gain experience in designing a training programme

To gain experience in working in a group and making presentations

To communicate effectively in writing

Skills developed: Analysis
Problem-solving
Decision-making
Design of a training programme
Presentation skills
Communication - verbal and written
Team-building

ROBERTSON ASSOCIATES PLC

Background

Robertson Associates plc is a large manufacturing and retailing company with a total staff of around 650. In the last two years the organisation has been experiencing a financial crisis. The number of customers has been declining and there have been many complaints about inefficiencies within the administration of the organisation. Because of the siting of the organisation and the generous salaries traditionally paid to staff, the rate of turnover among office and manufacturing staff has been fairly low.

Recent events

In an attempt to overcome the problems, there have been a number of changes in the senior management team within the last two months. A new General Manager has been brought in and some younger staff have been promoted to senior management level. A management working party has recently carried out an extensive global review of the organisation to identify the problem areas and has established that one of the priorities must be to modernise the administrative procedures by introducing a sophisticated office information system with desktop publishing facility. This plan has received a very mixed reception from the other Managers, some of whom have stated that they have managed successfully with their departmental word processors to date and that going on to a new networked and more complex system is unnecessary and likely to cause more problems than it solves.

Planned changes

The organisation currently has a computer which has been used for a fairly limited range of functions (eg payroll and accounting). Departments all have a word processing facility but there is no uniformity in equipment or word processing software. It is planned to extend the computerisation to include the entire ordering process, planning, budgeting and forecasting, and also the personnel records. The first step in this ambitious plan is to upgrade the computer and replace the different departmental word processing systems with terminals linked to the computer, which will provide sophisticated word processing software capable of integrating with the DTP facility. The computer supplier has assured the organisation that the software is "user friendly".

It is planned to retain the departmental structure of the organisation, with each department having its own terminals and at least one high-quality printer. There will be a total of between 80 and 90 employees using the word processing and DTP software, of whom 12 are Personal Assistants to the middle and senior management, 11 are Supervisors and the remainder are Word Processing Operators. None of them has any knowledge of the system to be introduced. Word of the management plans has leaked out to the office staff, from whom there is a very mixed reaction. A few are delighted, the majority are apprehensive about the new demands which the networked system and the new software will make on them, and a few are positively hostile at having to change systems.

ACTION

1 [This is designed as a group exercise with each group having about three members. It can, however, be undertaken as an individual exercise by omitting the second paragraph on page 124.]

You are the Training Section of the organisation and are asked to design a training package to meet the organisational needs associated with the introduction of the new word processing and DTP software. Your training budget is reasonably generous, without being over-lavish!

A meeting has been arranged for you to present the completed package to the Personnel Director and line Managers. You have been instructed to make your presentation 10-12 minutes in length.

Your training package should clearly state any assumptions that you have made over and above the information given in the case and should also include details on:

a the training objectives of the package

b who requires to be trained

c the length, mode of attendance and venue of the training, along with details of the ideal size of each training group

d who will undertake the training

e the content of the training programme and the learning methods which will be used

f the method(s) for evaluating the training package

2 Read the case study and, from the information it contains, write an essay analysing the difficulties and problems which the Training Section of Robertson Associates plc will have to overcome when planning a training programme for the introduction of the software.

This is not designed as a group exercise.

Case 8.5
Job design

General objectives: To develop an understanding of the factors which are present in well-designed jobs

To gain an understanding of some of the problems which can arise when jobs are badly designed

To analyse the case and recommend a solution to the current difficulties

Skills developed: Analysis
Problem-solving
Decision-making

JACKSON INSTRUMENTS PLC

Background

Jackson Instruments plc is a large manufacturing company located in a major industrial area. It is spread over four sites on three different industrial estates within a radius of five miles. The staff consists of approximately 500 clerical and secretarial staff as well as manufacturing staff. Over the past decade the company has grown slowly but steadily and has introduced considerable computerisation to the clerical function as well as a range of word processing systems for the secretarial staff. Relations between management and employees have always been fairly reasonable with the management style being a mixture of autocracy and paternalism.

The organisation has a job evaluation scheme for the manufacturing staff which was established many years ago. To date it has not extended this to the clerical and secretarial staff. At the current time there are five different salary grades on the clerical/secretarial scale. Promotion from Grade 1 to Grade 2 normally comes automatically after a period of about a year in post. Thereafter the criteria for promotion from one grade to another are much less clear and tend to depend on a recommendation from the Department Manager or, as often happens in the case of a Secretary, the change in status of the Manager.

The clerical and secretarial grades are as follows:

Grade 1   Junior (normally for first year in post after leaving school)
Grade 2   Clerical Assistant A, Typist
Grade 3   Clerical Assistant B, Word Processing Operator, Secretary
Grade 4   Senior Clerical Assistant, Supervisor, Senior Secretary
Grade 5   Section Head, Personal Assistant

There has always been considerable division of labour among clerical staff, with each employee being responsible for one specific part of the process. The organisation has four large typing pools for all general typing/word processing requirements (ie one in each building). All Managers, from middle management upwards, have their own Secretaries.

Current job design

When the computers and word processors were introduced there was no examination of job design. The relevant staff merely used a terminal where they would previously have carried out the job manually or used non-computerised equipment.

As a result, most of the clerical staff and all the Word Processing Operators worked for substantial periods on VDUs. There was a union agreement that all VDU operators should have a 15-minute break after 1½ hours continuous use of the VDUs and that no operator should use the equipment for more than four hours in any one day. In practice, however, this agreement has not been adhered to, largely because the shop steward has not appreciated the importance of factors other than job security and salary in relation to VDUs, and also because of the considerable pressure he is under in trying to cope with the many other union demands on his time.

Recent problems

The organisation has traditionally had a reputation of being a happy place in which to work. The situation has been changing, however, over the last few years with a growing discontent becoming obvious among many of the clerical and secretarial staff. The rate of turnover of staff has increased, although not as much as might have been the case had the salaries been less competitive with those of other organisations. There have been general complaints of a reduction in job satisfaction as well as increased stress, headaches, eyestrain and muscle pain.

The complaints have coincided with a push for increased productivity to retain the company's growth position, pressure to introduce a system of middle Managers sharing Secretaries and a demand for a substantial number of clerical and secretarial staff to use a wider range of software and/or more integrated packages. It has been noted that the number of customer complaints related to errors and delays in orders has been growing over the past few years.

Most of the staff in the typing pools use a word processor to some extent. In order to increase the rate of work turnover, the work has tended to be batched together by the Supervisor, with the Operators concentrating mainly on one type of work. A positive factor in this has been the reduced training costs as only those undertaking the more complex jobs require training in advanced text processing.

Recently there have been demands for staff in the typing pools to use other packages, with spreadsheets being the first to be requested. As a result, one operator from each pool was sent on a short course to learn the use of the package. The demand for use of the spreadsheet facility subsequently increased, requiring a further seven staff to learn to use the software. On this occasion the relevant staff were given copies of the equipment manual, which was backed up by tuition from the four staff who had been on the short course. Management has recently been heard to suggest the need to introduce graphics and desktop publishing packages.

In addition to the complaints already outlined above, there have been others from the clerical/secretarial staff about being merely a "cog in a machine" with little idea of whose work they are undertaking. They have also complained about the unfairness of vague statements blaming them for errors and delays and have pointed out that they are not aware that many errors and delays have occurred. Finally, staff have been heard to grumble about problems in using equipment. This has been particularly noticeable among those using the spreadsheet package who have also made representation to the Personnel Department about lack of remuneration for their increased skill.

Management action

In an attempt to reduce delays and improve control systems, senior management has decided to introduce a local area network which will link the computer equipment on all sites. This has brought pressure to standardise software and use compatible hardware.

At their last meeting, the management discussed the implications of the changes in job content which had recently occurred and which were likely to occur with the increased use of a wider range of software and/or the introduction of new software. During discussion it also became clear that there was a feeling that all clerical and secretarial staff should be able to use a word processor to at least a basic operator level and that secretarial staff should become less involved with routine typing and more involved in administration to provide a more effective service for management. It was decided to call in a team of Consultants to advise them on job re-design for clerical and secretarial staff.

ACTION

1 Examine the case study and outline the positive factors in the design of clerical/secretarial jobs in Jackson Instruments plc.

2 Outline the negative factors in the design of clerical/secretarial jobs in Jackson Instruments plc.

3 If you were the team of Consultants, what recommendations would you make to improve the job design in the organisation.

Case 8.6
Job evaluation

General objectives: To develop an understanding of job evaluation techniques

To develop an understanding of the problems which can arise in designing a job evaluation scheme

To develop an appreciation of some of the problems which can arise when evaluating a new type of job within an established evaluation scheme

To analyse the case and recommend a solution to the current difficulties

Skills developed: Analysis
Problem-solving
Decision-making

RAPIER PLC

Background

Rapier plc is a large organisation in the food retailing business with supermarkets/hypermarkets all over the country. It has traditionally been a very prosperous company and recently celebrated its centenary. It has always prided itself on providing excellent quality and variety at competitive prices.

Over the last 10 years it has experienced fluctuation in its fortunes. The first half of the decade saw a decrease in its annual profits and a reduction in its share of the market. There were various reasons for this, not the least of which were problems in the economy as a whole and a vigorous marketing campaign on the part of one of its competitors.

Major review

A few years ago the company carried out a major review of its position, resulting in two significant developments. The first development was the planned installation of a new computerised system which would integrate point-of-sale, financial control and document-production systems. The second development was the introduction of a programme to change the corporate culture to one with a much higher customer-care orientation and staff participation in decision-making. As part of this, Rapier has begun a series of training courses for check-out staff and retail supervisors in customer care.

Management recognised that changing the corporate culture was not an easy matter nor one which could be achieved over a short timescale. It was, however, something which management was determined to pursue for the long-term benefit of the company.

The decision was taken to phase the introduction of the new computerised system, beginning with head office and the hypermarkets. This brought upheavals to certain sections of the company and a number of job losses. Because of the relatively high turnover of staff, these were achieved mainly by natural wastage, with early retirement and a few voluntary redundancies making up the remainder. The job content and procedures for many of the staff who remained were altered considerably and the division between traditionally blue-collar and white-collar jobs became blurred.

Proposed job evaluation scheme

Throughout the changes, in line with its policy of increased staff participation, the management held regular meetings with the trade unions. One of the results of the discussions has been the recent proposal to extend and integrate the current job evaluation scheme to include clerical, secretarial and administrative staff as well as those who were already on the scheme. The scheme is based on the points rating scheme and has been in operation for a number of years for all retail staff and manual workers.

To carry out the extension of the job evaluation scheme, an additional three members - to represent the three new areas to be incorporated - have been drafted on to the existing Job Evaluation Committee. This Committee has the responsibility of overseeing the scheme, reviewing existing gradings and allocating new gradings where appropriate. The Joint Management/Trade Union Committee also expressed the desire to extend the scheme further in the near future to incorporate the different levels of management. The Job Evaluation Committee was specifically asked to give consideration to this future development when incorporating the clerical, secretarial and administrative jobs.

The following sections give details of the current job evaluation scheme.

Current job evaluation factors

Skill

1 Education
   The general educational qualifications required to perform the job.

2 **Technical training**
The specific technical training required to perform the job.

3 **Experience**
The time period required before an employee can perform the job satisfactorily. This includes previous experience as well as the time taken for a new member of staff to become familiar with the organisation and the specific requirements of the job.

4 **Initiative**
The extent to which the job requires the employee to use initiative.

Effort

5 **Physical skills**
The extent to which the job requires physical effort and stamina from the employee.

6 **Mental skills**
The extent to which the job requires mental effort from the employee.

7 **Visual demands**
The extent to which the job requires visual effort from the employee.

Responsibility

8 **Equipment**
The value of equipment and the degree of risk of damage to this which is within the responsibility of the employee.

9 **Materials and non-capital resources**
The level of responsibility for materials and other non-capital resources (eg human resources).

10 **Safety**
The degree to which safety factors, other than the normal duties of any employee, are a major consideration of the job.

Working conditions

11 **Unsocial hours**
The extent to which the job requires shiftwork and other unsocial hours.

12 **Environmental conditions**
The extent to which adverse temperature, noise, dirt, etc, impinge on the job.

13 **Boredom**
The extent to which the job involves tasks which are highly repetitive and boring and the extent to which a high degree of accuracy is required.

Pointage and weighting

Under the current scheme all 13 factors have a possible rating of between 0 and 5. The factors are weighted according to their importance with factors under the headings of "skill" and "responsibility" having a weighting of two as against a weighting of one for all the others.

Evaluating a job is therefore undertaken as follows:

- Allocate a rating of 0-5 for each of the 13 factors.
- Double the score for factors 1-4 and 8-10.
- The job score is obtained by adding the weighted total of each factor.

The job grading is obtained by comparing the job score with the predetermined grading scores. The grading will, of course, determine the salary scale on which the employee is placed.

Extract from agreed gradings currently in operation

Factor	Packer R	Packer WR	Check-out Assistant R	Check-out Assistant WR	Retail Supervisor R	Retail Supervisor WR	Stock Supervisor R	Stock Supervisor WR
1	(0)	0	(0)	0	(1)	2	(1)	2
2	(0)	0	(1)	2	(2)	4	(2)	4
3	(1)	2	(2)	4	(3)	6	(3)	6
4	(1)	2	(1)	2	(3)	6	(3)	6
5	(3)	3	(2)	2	(2)	2	(2)	2
6	(1)	1	(2)	2	(3)	3	(3)	3
7	(1)	1	(3)	3	(3)	3	(2)	2
8	(1)	2	(2)	4	(3)	6	(2)	4
9	(2)	4	(2)	4	(3)	6	(3)	6
10	(2)	4	(1)	2	(3)	6	(4)	8
11	(4)	4	(4)	4	(4)	4	(4)	4
12	(3)	3	(2)	2	(2)	2	(3)	3
13	(3)	3	(4)	4	(2)	2	(2)	2
Totals		29		35		52		52

Key: R = rating   WR = weighted rating

Gradings   1 = totals up to 33
           2 = 34-43
           3 = 44-53
           4 = 54-63
           5 = 64-73

Packer   = grade 1   Check-out Assistant = grade 2
Retail Supervisor   = grade 3   Stock Supervisor   = grade 3

Brief job descriptions

Packer   Employee who transports goods from the storeroom to the sales floor and packs the shelves - no formal or technical qualifications required

Check-out Assistant Employee who is in charge of a check-out point - no formal qualifications required; some technical training given

Retail Supervisor   Employee who supervises Check-out Assistants, advises on problems and occasionally provides relief at check-out - some formal qualifications required; technical and supervisory skills required

Stock Supervisor   Employee who is responsible for supervision of storeroom and storeroom staff - some formal qualifications required; technical and supervisory skills required

ACTION

1 What ratings and grading would be given to the following jobs, based on the brief job descriptions shown beside them?

   Clerk   Employee who undertakes routine clerical work in the relevant department - educational qualifications at O level/grade required - some technical training including VDU operation required

   Personal Assistant   Personal Assistant/Secretary to Departmental Manager - educational qualifications at A level or H grade; considerable technical training including VDU operation required

   Administrative Assistant Professional Assistant in a relevant department - educational and appropriate technical qualifications to HND/degree level required

Assistant Manager   Assistant Manager of a Department - educational and technical qualifications to HND/degree level and professional qualification required; considerable experience at professional assistant level required

2 What problems, if any, did you experience in trying to give a rating and grading to the jobs listed in question 1? In your opinion what were the causes of these problems? What recommendations would you make to resolve the problems?

3 From your knowledge and from analysis of the above case study, discuss the advantages of moving towards an integrated job evaluation scheme and examine the problems which are likely to arise.

Case 8.7
Ergonomics, health and safety

General objectives: To gain an understanding of some of the ergonomic, health and safety issues related to VDUs

To analyse the case and identify some of the likely causes of the ergonomics, health and safety problems

To recommend a course of action to reduce or overcome the problems

Skills developed: Analysis
Problem-solving
Decision-making

MAXWELL PETROLEUM (UK) PLC

Background

Maxwell Petroleum (UK) plc is part of a large multinational group with its main headquarters in the United States. There are two centres of operation in the United Kingdom. The Exploration Centre, which is based just north of Aberdeen, and the United Kingdom headquarters in London. The Exploration Centre is mainly concerned with exploration in the North Sea and subsequent management of the process of getting the oil from the oilrigs to the refinery on the mainland.

The Aberdeen Centre

The building in Aberdeen, which was opened 18 months ago and replaced an older building, is modern and circular in design. The office space is on the perimeter of the building and has large areas of slightly tinted glass from floor to ceiling. The Aberdeen complex comprises 300 staff, 70 of whom are of managerial status with the remainder falling into the categories of professional, technical, clerical and secretarial.

It is organisational policy that, with the exception of one or two Senior Managers on each site, secretarial services are shared between two or three people - if possible within the same department. Both locations recognise the right of their employees to belong to a trade union. Overall, among the clerical and secretarial staff, there is a 52% union membership, the principal union being the MSF.

Recent developments

Within the last few months, the UK company has experienced a number of problems. The most serious of these were due to a decline in the extent of the North Sea exploration. Further problems were caused by the general world recession and the introduction of a new, integrated and streamlined computer system which reduced the requirement for clerical and secretarial staff. The company recently announced the necessity for significant job losses and introduced a voluntary redundancy policy. At the same time management stated that, in the event of the target for job losses not being met, there would be no alternative but to consider introducing compulsory redundancies. Senior management has also recently been considering rationalising resources between Aberdeen and London.

Management held discussions with the trade unions prior to the announcements on job losses. The unions agreed with some reluctance to the policy of voluntary redundancies but were much less happy with the possibility of subsequent compulsory redundancies. They have warned the Management that such a policy is likely to lead to industrial action. To date the number of staff accepting voluntary redundancy has been low and the general uncertainty coupled with the other changes in the organisation have had an effect on morale among staff at both locations.

Temperature problems

In general, the Aberdeen staff liked the new building, which looked attractive and was well equipped. Unfortunately, fairly shortly after the plans for the building were passed, there was an increase in the staff at Aberdeen which resulted in the building being less spacious than had originally been planned. The situation is likely to improve in the longer term, however, when the main exploration stage is completed.

One thing which many staff complained about, however, was the temperature. The building is air-conditioned and cool air is circulated when the thermostat indicates that the temperature has reached a certain point. Staff in specific areas regularly complained of being too cold. The cause of the problem seemed to be that if one section of the office got very warm, the air-conditioning for the entire office space came on. Staff in the other sections which had not become overheated suddenly found cold air blowing down on them. The problem could not be solved by opening windows in the warm areas since the windows were all sealed units.

Attempts were being made solve the problem by raising the temperature at which the air-conditioning switched on. The situation improved for those in the cooler areas but staff in the warmer areas were then too hot. The sections which tended to overheat were the south-facing areas and a west-facing area where there was a concentration of computer terminals.

Computer problems

Other problems occurred with the new, integrated computer system. The first of these was a breakdown problem which happened three times in quick succession. As one might expect, the breakdowns all occurred at periods of high computer usage when there were urgent jobs with tight deadlines. On two of the three occasions, staff lost a lot of the information which they had been inputting. This resulted in their having to work the entire weekend to re-input the data and complete the job. The fact that they had only fairly recently undergone training on the new system and were still unfamiliar with certain procedures, had lengthened the time it took them to finish the work. They had been very unhappy about the whole situation, particularly as they had also been complaining bitterly about the slow response time of the system at certain periods in the day. Management promised to investigate the situation and eliminate both problems as quickly as possible.

Increased absences

Another area which was causing concern was the increased incidence of staff having short periods of sick leave. In most cases this only amounted to one or two days and tended to occur mainly among staff using computers. The staff absences, however, caused problems for the relevant departments because of their high workloads. What tended to happen was that the other departmental staff who were able to use the equipment were required to work overtime to get the jobs completed. They were very unhappy about this situation and complained that they were getting more than their share of the additional work which, given that their own jobs required them to spend much of each day on the computer, meant that they were having virtually no break from the computer.

General health problems

There had always been some staff complaints of eyestrain but, again, the incidence of such complaints had risen over the past year. This occurred despite the fact that the new building had tinted windows and uplighting and that all staff were recommended to have their eyes tested before using a VDU. Informal discussions with staff highlighted that these tests were not always happening. A number of staff were very vociferous in their complaints and stated that their eyesight had deteriorated since they had started using the terminals so much. In the case of other staff the complaints about eyestrain were more intermittent but tended mainly to occur after periods of intensive work.

The organisational nurse reported to the management her concern at the significant increase in complaints about headaches. The headaches were occurring not only among terminal users but also among the staff in general. During the discussions, one or two of the staff had also mentioned that they were experiencing some difficulty in sleeping. The nurse gave details in her report about two members of staff who had come to see her about a facial rash which they had noticed on several occasions. When questioned, they said that the rash had disappeared within a few hours of their finishing work for the day. The nurse had inquired about the possibility of a build-up of static being the cause of the problem but that did not seem to be likely since special care had been taken when purchasing the carpeting to ensure that it had anti-static properties.

The nurse reported serious concern about one terminal operator who had come to see her recently because of pain in her arms. The woman said that she had been experiencing the pain for some time but that it had got much worse within the last month. The situation had deteriorated to such an extent that she was now finding it almost impossible to use the keyboard. The operator said that she was very worried about her job if the problem did not clear up soon. She asked the nurse whether or not it was likely that she would be able to get any compensation from the company if she were unable to carry on with her job. The nurse indicated that she was unable to make any comment about compensation but recommended her to see a doctor at once.

ACTION

1 Read the case and identify any problems being experienced by Maxwell Petroleum which relate to ergonomics, health and safety.

2 Why do you think the nurse is seriously concerned about the terminal operator who is complaining of pain in her arms? What are the likely causes of such a problem?

3 From your theoretical knowledge, what are the potential causes of the other health problems being experienced by staff of Maxwell Petroleum? To what extent are these causes likely to be found in the Aberdeen complex?

4 What action would you recommend should be taken by the management of Maxwell Petroleum to remedy the problems?

Case 8.8
Negotiation role-play exercise

General objectives: To reinforce understanding of negotiation procedures

To gain experience of working in a team

To develop negotiation skills

To give an appreciation of some of the problems which tend to occur during the negotiating process

Skills developed: Analysis
Problem-solving
Decision-making
Verbal communication
Team-building
Negotiation skills

WESTERN COLLEGE

General information

At Western College there is currently a dispute between the staff and students on one of the courses. The problem has arisen over timetabling. The lecturer for one of the final year subjects has recently been seconded to a national education body for one day a week (ie every Monday) to develop a new national course. He is scheduled to take up his appointment at the beginning of February, which is in two weeks' time, and the secondment is for the remainder of the session. As a result he is no longer able to lecture to the group on their first hour on Monday (ie from 1000-1100 hours).

The Course Leader has intimated to the students that there is no-one else available who has a knowledge of the complete syllabus. They inquired whether or not the lecturer could go on a day other than a Monday but this had not proved possible. There appears, therefore, to be no alternative but to reschedule the class. The subject has three lecture hours and one tutorial hour per week.

There are only two possible times within the 0900-1700 day when the students, the member of staff and a suitable room are free - one is on a Friday from 1600-1700 hours and the other is on a Tuesday from 1200-1300 hours. The Course

Leader has ruled out the Tuesday because there is a lecture already scheduled on that day from 1100-1200 hours and most students have a tutorial at 1300 hours. A substantial number of the students also have a double hour from 1400-1600 hours. The lecturer is not keen to take the class on a Tuesday as he would have no lunch break. It must be said that neither the lecturer nor the students are enthusiastic about the thought of the Friday afternoon class.

Student complaints of excessive workload

The students, in discussion with the Course Leader, took the opportunity to complain about what they considered to be the excessive amount of work they are being asked to undertake. This has been aggravated by the fact that two lecturers (including the one already mentioned) would not recommend any specific reading references. The reason for this was that a substantial number of books and journals, which had been recommended to that particular class at the beginning of the year, had disappeared from the Library shelves within 12 hours of their being mentioned in the lecture or, in the case of a number of journals, had had the relevant pages torn out. Investigation by library staff showed no record of the missing material being out on loan.

The students complained, firstly, that they had to spend so much time searching the library shelves for their own references and, secondly, that they were sure they often missed the best ones. The two staff retorted that, if they gave references, there would be a tendency to get stereotyped answers and, in any case, they had seen little evidence to date of hard work from the majority of the students.

ACTION

Each team should meet as a group to prepare for the negotiation. The preparation should include:

- discussion on who should take the important role of the team leader/co-ordinator
- what negotiation strategies and tactics should be adopted
- what is going to be the team's initial bargaining stance
- what are the team's priorities
- what are the various issues on which the team is prepared to give way or "go down"
- what might the other side want
- what might the other side offer
- what response should be given to the different courses of action which the other side might adopt

After the preparation, the two sides should come together for the negotiation session.

Notes for Tutor

Before the negotiation exercise can be run, it is desirable to produce a confidential brief for the staff and one for the students. Both briefs should contain a number of details which are not known by the other side. This "confidential" information should complicate the negotiation and make it less easy for the two sides to reach an agreement. This can be done by getting one side to raise a new issue which is likely to be contentious or by making sure that obvious "solutions" to the problems outlined in the general information are not viable propositions. Remember, however, to leave some room for the two sides to manoeuvre, otherwise there will be nothing to negotiate! It is suggested that some of the information given should be related to the issue of the class scheduling but it is a good idea if other information is not. Experience indicates that staff and students seldom meet to discuss one issue without other issues being raised by both groups.

A good number for each negotiation team is three. A team of two does not bring the same difficulty of control when discussion gets heated while four or more tends to mean that at least one person takes little or no part in the negotiation discussions. Another problem with more than four is that it becomes *very* difficult to prevent the situation arising where everyone is talking at once and as a result no-one is listening.

Remember to stress to students the importance of *listening*. Experience of negotiation training sessions indicates that quite a regular occurrence is for one team to make a concession which in effect provides the solution to the problems. The members of the other team, however, are so intent on following the former course of the discussion and thinking of their next moves that no-one in the team is listening properly and therefore they do not recognise that the solution has been given to them. In such instances it is quite common for the debate and argument to continue for some time and the chance of a solution to be lost.

Another aspect to stress is the use of adjournments to allow for team discussion (eg if one team wants to discuss a proposal made by the other side, or if one team wants to discuss what proposal they might put forward, or if they want to discuss how their side should react to the difficult/unexpected situation in which they find themselves).

You may have to intervene occasionally if there is a prolonged period of stalemate. Watch, however, that you do not intervene too soon. If intervention is necessary, try to help the teams to work out for themselves how they might break the deadlock. Beware of imposing your own ideas!

SECTION 9
INTEGRATED CASES

In the study of any subject it is vital to gain an understanding not only of the constituent parts but also of the subject as a whole and the relationships between constituent parts. For this reason, Section 9 is given over to cases which bring integration to some of the areas examined in earlier sections.

The aim of the section goes beyond this, however. Case studies are designed to provide a simulation of real-life situations. Since problems in real-life seldom have only one causal factor, it is important that students are exposed to complex situations and gain some experience in handling complexity through analysis, identification of causes and the making of recommendations for overcoming the problems. It is hoped that, by working through the cases in this section, students will begin to build skill in the handling of complexity.

Case 9.1
General administrative systems

General objectives: To analyse the case study and identify the problems which it contains

To gain an understanding of the complex nature of some problems

To develop skills in report-writing

Skills developed: Analysis
Problem-solving
Decision-making
Report-writing
Communication

MARLEY AGRICULTURAL CENTRE

Background

Marley Agricultural Centre is an organisation which services the agricultural needs of the area in which it is situated and the five adjacent areas, by providing specialist agricultural advice and training courses at advanced level. It is sited on a large estate and comprises one main Victorian building, which was originally a stately home, surrounded by a number of smaller buildings - some of which also date from the Victorian era while others are fairly modern, prefabricated-style buildings.

The main building houses some centralised administrative facilities and each of the smaller buildings has its own administrative support staff to meet the document production needs of several professional staff. In most cases the support staff consists of an Audio Typist and/or a Clerk Typist. Because of the pressure on support staff, the professional staff, mainly College Lecturers or Specialist Agricultural Advisors, have to undertake the majority of their own administration.

As with most organisations, Marley Agricultural Centre is experiencing severe financial pressures and the Governing Body of the Centre has recently taken the policy decision to introduce economic charges for all advisory services provided to the farming community. In a document circulated to all staff, the Governing

Body has stressed the need to maximise efficiency and to improve the public image of the Centre.

Departmental meeting

One department in the Centre is the Animal Production Advisory Department. It has a Head of Department, a professional staff of 15 and two administrative support staff, one of whom works a shorter day (0900-1500 hours) because of family commitments. The Head of Department, Eric Dean, called a departmental meeting last week to discuss the recent circular from the Governing Body. He was greatly annoyed at the unexplained absence from the meeting of four of the professional staff, only one of whom was found to be in the building.

Considerable time was lost in trying to locate the other three members and Nora Watt, the part-time typist, had had to interrupt an urgent job. She had been telephoning 30 delegates, scheduled to attend a seminar on the following day, who had been asked to report to the wrong hotel.

Fred Robb, a fairly new member of the professional staff, was eventually tracked down in the Soil Science Department, which was in another building. There was no trace of the other two missing members who were later found to have been out on visits that day.

The electronic mail system

All four missing members later disclaimed any knowledge of the meeting. The notice of the meeting had taken the form of an electronic memo to all departmental staff. When the meeting did eventually start, there was a lot of discussion among the professional staff about the wisdom of using this method of communication, and two other Advisors admitted that they only knew of the meeting because of a conversation with one of their colleagues.

It was thought that the problem was due to the siting of the terminals. The Centre had networked all the buildings. In the Animal Production Advisory Department there were three terminals installed in a room at the end of the corridor nearest the main building.

The general discussion highlighted the fact that a number of staff did not consider that the electronic mail system was at all helpful to them. They stated that they could see no advantage in the system, particularly since they had heard about some of the recent problems experienced by departmental staff in accessing the system and in printing. They added that they had neither the time to learn how to operate the system nor the time to waste trying to use it. Two members of staff said that they had gone to a one-day training session run by the suppliers. At the time they had found the course quite enjoyable, if somewhat confusing in places, and had thought that, when they got a system installed, it would be most useful.

This had not proved to be the case when, two months later, the equipment at last arrived and they had started to use it. They had experienced difficulty remembering some of the things they had covered on the course and, when they had tried to look up one or two things in the manual, they had found it impossible to follow. When this point was made, another member of staff, Eric, who it was well known did not "get on" with the Computer Facilities Manager, responded by making a sarcastic comment about the lack of ability of the Computer Facilities Manager to recommend a system which could possibly be of any use to the departments.

The complaints continued and even those who made frequent use of the system pointed out that it was often quicker to re-key a document than to hunt through numerous disks for the file. One Advisor commented with feeling that she had wasted half an hour the previous day looking for a statistical report. When she found it, the file could not be accessed as it had been damaged. She had ended up by having to re-key the entire nine-page document!

One of the professional staff told the meeting that she had contacted the Computer Facilities Manager about the printing problems and asked if the department could get another printer; she had added the request that they be given a fast, good-quality laser printer which would be of particular benefit to them in their consultancy work. The Computer Facilities Manager had replied that he *could* give them another printer - but not the laser printer she wanted, because of the cost. He had told her, however, that he was planning to recommend that all buildings retain only a small, fairly basic printer and, at the same time, be networked to a centralised laser printing facility for high-quality printing. When Eric heard of this he was very angry and stated that *he* was Head of the department and would decide what level of printing facility they had.

Client complaints

At the meeting, Eric Dean made special mention of some client complaints which had recently been received. One fairly new client had been angry when he had received a letter addressed to someone else - particularly when he realised that it contained a specific reference to his contact with the Centre.

The following day Eric had received another letter from a client, this time complaining about the tone of a letter written by one of the professional staff in the department and of his subsequent rudeness on the telephone. When challenged, the member of staff strongly refuted the claim, stating that he had merely been "businesslike" in the letter and had certainly not been rude on the telephone. He added that this particular client was well known for being rather "difficult". The member of staff finally did admit, however, that he had perhaps been a bit abrupt on the telephone as he was frantically trying to get an overdue article off to the monthly farming magazine.

Eric was alarmed at this last statement, because he knew that the article was the third in a series of articles which the magazine had asked the Centre to provide in return for their sponsorship of a major research programme within the department. There had been some problems in meeting the deadlines for the first two articles and the magazine had already threatened to withdraw the sponsorship.

Management meeting

At the management meeting later that week, George Clark, the Head of the Soil Science Department, commented on the need for at least one upgraded computer terminal for each department. Eric came in right away and stated that he thought this was unnecessary as no-one in his Department was having any problems with the power of the terminals. George immediately said that he was very surprised at Eric's reaction because he must be aware that Fred Robb, to whom George had been speaking recently, was having exactly that kind of problem and was finding that this was hindering him in his work. George added that Fred had asked for his support in getting upgraded terminals. Eric was furious and made a note to have words with Fred as he knew nothing of this problem.

ACTION

1 Read the case study and identify the problems which are being experienced by the Marley Agricultural Centre.

2 Analyse these problems and examine their causes, identifying those relating to general administrative systems and those relating to other factors.

3 Recommend a course of action which should be taken to remedy the situation. Make sure that your recommendations are specific as to what has to be done and by whom.

Case 9.2
In-tray exercise

General objectives: To gain experience in the problems of time management

To analyse the case study and identify problems

To gain an understanding of the problem of managing complexity

To develop presentational skills

Skills developed: Analysis
Problem-solving
Decision-making
Time management
Presentational skills
Verbal communication

STATIONERY SUPPLIERS (EDINBURGH) LTD

Background

Stationery Suppliers (Edinburgh) Ltd is a subsidiary company of Stationery Suppliers (London) plc, which has another subsidiary company in Canada. The three companies have close ties which necessitate a considerable amount of travelling from one site to another. Stationery Suppliers (London) plc has direct computer links with the Canadian subsidiary and also with the smaller computer in Edinburgh, which has a number of terminals attached to it. Stationery Suppliers (Edinburgh) is responsible for the supply of stationery to the whole of Scotland and to customers in Denmark.

The Communications Department is split into three sections under the Communications Manager, George Watson. The first section is the data processing section which is the responsibility of Donald Barr, the Data Processing Administrator. The second section is the secretarial servicing section, including word processing, which is the responsibility of Ruth Baxter, the Secretarial Administrator. The third section is the responsibility of Robert Jackson, who also acts as Assistant Communications Manager. In this capacity Robert Jackson has also had quite a number of other tasks delegated to him by George Watson. One of these additional tasks is the responsibility for the subsidiary company's motor insurance.

There are two trade unions involved with the company, of which APEX is by far the larger with fairly substantial representation among the various levels of administrative staff as well as some at lower management level. The APEX Trade Union Representative is James Cameron, who is one of the clerical staff in the Communications Department.

The data processing section is under pressure at present because of a shortage of staff. Five weeks ago Bill McTavish, a Systems Analyst, left to take up a post which represented a promotion in another organisation. The following week Jennifer Davis, one of the Data Processing Assistants, also left as her husband had taken up a new post in the south of England. As yet there have been no replacements.

Over the past few months there has been some trouble in the word processing section from which temporary relief cover has always been obtained if any of the Personal Assistants is absent. The claim by the union for such staff to have a temporary upgrading during the period was turned down by management. Since then the word processing staff have been very discontented and unco-operative.

The Word Processing Supervisor, Jean McCallum, recently has been granted permission to take early retirement to look after her elderly mother, who is house-bound and in failing health. George Watson, having looked around the section and discussed the matter with Ruth Baxter, is considering approaching Anne MacLeod, one of the Word Processing Operators, with a view to recommending her for promotion to Word Processing Supervisor.

The date is Monday, 18 May and the time is 0900 hours. George Watson has just returned from a week's conference in Ohio, USA, on Electronic Data Interchange. There are a number of items in his in-tray awaiting attention.

The following is a section of the organisational chart of Stationery Suppliers (Edinburgh) Ltd.

STATIONERY SUPPLIERS (EDINBURGH) LTD
(Section of organisation chart)

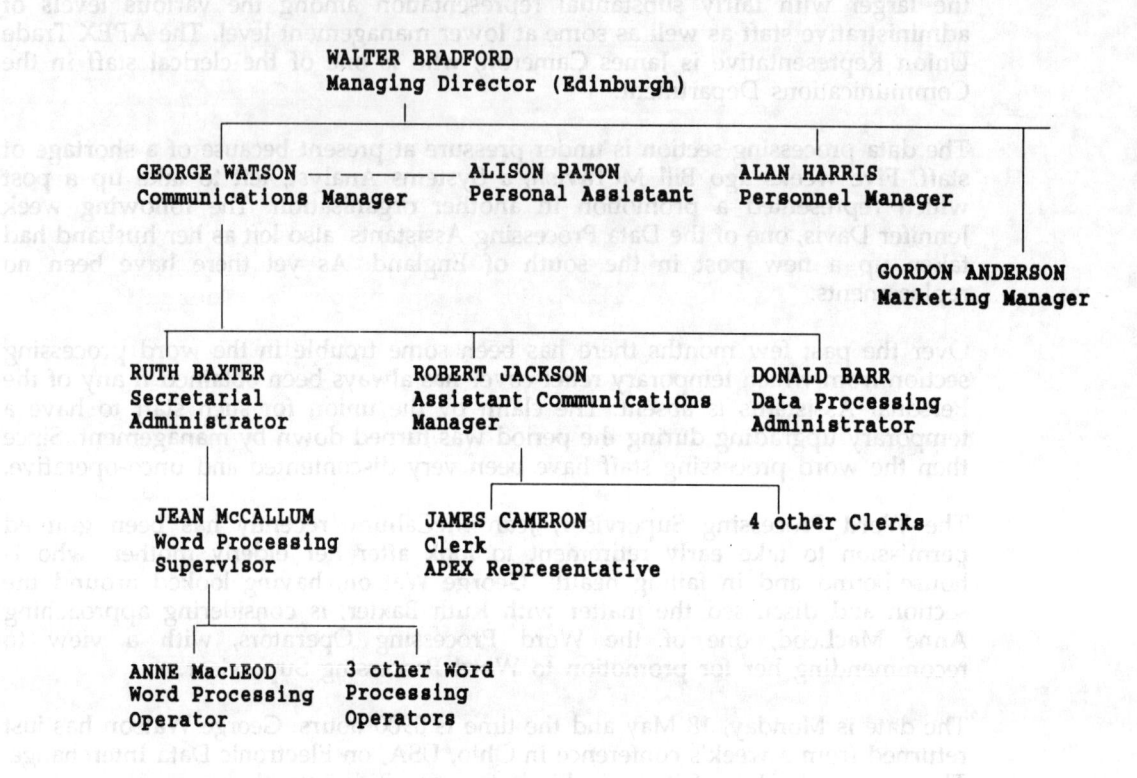

```
                    WALTER BRADFORD
                    Managing Director (Edinburgh)
    _____|_____
    |                       |                       |
GEORGE WATSON ————— ALISON PATON            ALAN HARRIS
Communications Manager  Personal Assistant   Personnel Manager

                                            GORDON ANDERSON
                                            Marketing Manager

    _____|_____
    |                   |                   |
RUTH BAXTER         ROBERT JACKSON       DONALD BARR
Secretarial         Assistant Communications   Data Processing
Administrator       Manager              Administrator

    |                   |                   |
JEAN McCALLUM       JAMES CAMERON        4 other Clerks
Word Processing     Clerk
Supervisor          APEX Representative

    |                   |
ANNE MacLEOD        3 other Word
Word Processing     Processing
Operator            Operators
```

Item 1

Memo dated 15 May from Mrs Jean McCallum on the subject of "unacceptable rudeness":

I feel compelled to make a strong complaint about the conduct of Mr Robert Jackson. Because of a virus on the disk on which the price list is stored, we were unable to produce the monthly update due today. I explained the situation to Mr Jackson and undertook to have the re-input of the price-list completed by Wednesday, 20 May. This will involve considerable extra effort on the part of staff, who will be one short on Tuesday as Anne will be attending an interview on that day.

The reaction of Mr Jackson was totally unreasonable. I do not use bad language myself, nor do any of my family or friends, and I am not prepared to tolerate it from anyone, especially when I am being helpful and obliging.

I should be grateful if you would convey this to Mr Jackson and instruct him as to his attitude and language in the future.

Item 2

Memo dated 15 May from Gordon Anderson, Marketing Manager, on the subject of "Regional School Stationery Account":

Further to my Memo of yesterday, the Region has given us until Wednesday (ie 20 May) to get their outstanding orders delivered.

I will expect to hear from you on Monday.

Item 3

Memo dated 15 May from James Cameron, APEX Representative, on the subject of "New Working Practices":

It would appear from certain actions by the Data Processing staff (namely the use of the computer links to correspond with London and Canada) plus information which has come to my attention about plans to instal new telecommunications links, that the organisation is planning a radical change in the working systems. Such a change would have major repercussions on the jobs of APEX members.

As APEX Representative, I consider it imperative that we hold discussions immediately, as my members will be unable to co-operate with any changes in their working practices which have not been previously agreed with the union.

Item 4

Telephone message dated 15 May (time 0910 hours) taken by L Findlay from Ruth Baxter:

Mrs Baxter's mother-in-law died unexpectedly last night. She will be off today and Monday (day of funeral).

Item 5

Memo from Alan Harris, Personnel Manager, on 14 May on the subject of "Word Processing Training":

I had occasion yesterday to see Miss Anne MacLeod, one of your WP Operators, on a personal matter. During our discussion she mentioned that the training she had had on the new office information system was, to quote her words, "pretty useless". The training was carried out by the WP Supervisor who, according to Anne, has a limited knowledge of the system, is very haphazard in her teaching methods and positively discourages any of the girls from experimenting or attempting to improve the established procedures.

I tried very tactfully to raise some of these points with Mrs McCallum but received a hostile reaction. In her opinion, Anne is becoming "too big for her boots" and is merely trying to create trouble. (I have subsequently learned that Mrs McCallum reprimanded Anne in front of the others on Monday for what appears, on the surface at least, to have been a very trivial matter. I understand that Anne took strong exception to this and a "shouting match" developed between the 2 of them!)

Could we meet in my office on Tuesday at 1030 hours to discuss the situation?

Item 6

Telephone message dated 15 May from Jean Sim, Secretary of the local branch of the British Management Association:

Mr Steve Mathers, the speaker organised for the next meeting on Monday, 25 May, cannot come but would be free on Monday, 22 June, the date you are due to speak. Can you exchange dates? Please phone.

The short committee meeting after the meeting on 25 May is now confirmed.

Telephone call

While George was reading through his mail, the telephone rang. It was Walter Bradford, the Managing Director. He first of all commented on how good it was to have George back and asked him how he had enjoyed the conference and had he got useful information?

Walter asked George if he could come to his office right then to read over the paper Walter was proposing to put to the next management meeting. Walter said that it was important that he got this out by lunch time since, as George knew, he was off to Canada later that day. Walter indicated that he wanted George's comments prior to sending out the paper.

Walter finished by saying that he was, of course, still remembering their 2 pm appointment that afternoon.

Item 7

Telephone message dated 15 May from John Ross, Motor Department of Northrop Insurance Brokers Ltd:

Urgent reminder that the premium for the company's motor policy, due on Tuesday a week ago, has not been received. Mr Ross warned that "days of grace" are not permitted under motor policies and that the temporary certificate which accompanied the renewal notice will expire next Wednesday. It will therefore be illegal to use the vehicles after that date unless the premium is paid. The brokers, of course, cannot release the full certificates until the premium is paid.

Item 8

Memo dated 14 May from Gordon Anderson, Marketing Manager, regarding "Regional School Stationery Account":

I received an irate letter today from the Regional Finance Director threatening to cancel our contract for the regional school stationery. They have contacted me twice within the last 6 weeks to complain of the delay in delivery of their orders. On both occasions the problem lay with very slow order processing in your section. As you were in London on each occasion, I contacted Robert Jackson who promised faithfully to remedy the situation. It appears that nothing has been done and we are now faced with this ultimatum.

Could you please investigate the matter <u>urgently</u> and let me know what steps you have taken to ensure that the problem does not arise again. Meanwhile I will contact the Region and try to placate them, as we <u>cannot</u> afford to lose the contract.

Item 9

Memo dated 13 May from Walter Bradford, Managing Director, regarding "Teleconferencing proposal":

I have unexpectedly to go to Canada for 4 days next week and will be catching the 7 pm flight to Toronto on Monday.

Could I therefore see you on Monday at 2 pm instead of Wednesday to discuss this proposal of yours to introduce teleconferencing. You had better bring with you the preliminary financial breakdown of costs and savings.

Item 10

Memo dated 13 May from Donald Barr, DP Administrator, regarding "Computer Servicing":

Although the computer is operational at present, over the last 3 years we have had a series of breakdowns. This has caused us major problems, particularly since we are already 2 members of staff short. Not only do ABM seem unable to get to the root of the problem, but we are having to wait much longer than the agreed 4 hours for the arrival of the engineer. (On 2 occasions the waiting time has been just over 24 hours.) My complaints to ABM are bringing no improvement. Perhaps some action from you would have more effect.

I would be grateful if you could look into this as soon as possible.

Is there any word of when we will get the replacements for Jennifer Davis and Bill McTavish who left 4 and 5 weeks ago respectively? I haven't seen any advertisements in the newspapers. Do you know if Personnel has put them in yet?

Item 11

Telephone message dated 14 May about Alison Paton, Personal Assistant:

Miss Paton has bronchitis. She will be absent for the next 2 weeks. She hopes to return on Thursday 28 May.

Item 12

An information sheet about a one-day seminar at the Reid Business School on:

INFORMATION MANAGEMENT

The date of the seminar is Wednesday, 27 May, the cost is £100 (inclusive of lunch and VAT) and the tear-off slip has to be completed and returned, along with an appropriate cheque, by Wednesday, 20 May.

Item 13

Letter dated 7 May from R L Palmer, the Director of the Victoria Leisure Centre:

Ref: Miss Anne MacLeod

Miss Anne MacLeod has applied for the post of secretary in our Finance Department. We would be grateful if you could give us information about her ability and character as well as your opinion as to her suitability for the post.

Since the interviews for the vacancy will be held on the morning of Tuesday, 19 May, an early response would be appreciated. We enclose a stamped, addressed envelope for your reply.

Item 14

Memo dated 11 May from Alison Paton regarding an appointment for a Mr Charles White:

I am very sorry but I completely forgot to record that I had arranged for Mr Charles White (a PhD student) to call today at 2.15 pm in connection with his research, to discuss with you the effect that the growth and development of information technology is having on the job of a manager.

I have apologised to him and arranged for him to call again and see you on Monday, 18 May, at 2.15 pm.

(Charles White is the son of the Managing Director of George Adamson plc from whom I know we are trying to get a major order.)

Telephone call

The telephone rang again. This time it was from Alan Harris, the Personnel Officer, asking George if he could send over urgently the information to put in the advertisement for replacement of the two computer staff who left four or five weeks ago. Alan reminded George that the advertisement would have to be with the newspaper by noon tomorrow if it were to catch the special job advertisement supplement which was issued each Friday.

Alan pointed out that, since George was going away for a month's holiday in a few weeks' time, it was important that the advertisement appeared this week if the interviews were to be held before the summer holiday period. He reminded George that he had already received two requests for this information and had not responded to either.

Item 15

Memo dated 11 May from Alison Paton regarding the analysis you wanted of the travelling expenses:

Donald Barr called and asked me to leave a message for you to say that he will be unable to provide the full analysis of the travelling expenses for the past 3 months until Tuesday, 19 May, because of the repeated breakdowns of the computer plus the delay in receiving expenses claim forms from 2 Managers.

ACTION

1 Take the role of George Watson. Read the items in your in-tray and then decide:

   a how you would deal with each of them, and
   b in which order you would deal with them.

2 Analyse the information and identify the problems which exist in Stationery Suppliers (Edinburgh) Ltd.

3 If you had been a Consultant called into the organisation, what recommendations would you have made to remedy the problems?

Case 9.3
Management of change

General objectives: To analyse the case and identify problems related to change management

To gain an appreciation of the complexity of managing change

To develop presentational skills

Skills developed: Analysis
Problem-solving
Decision-making
Presentation skills
Verbal communication

COPYMATICS PLC

Background

Copymatics plc is a medium-sized organisation which manufactures and distributes photocopying equipment. Traditionally it has been very much involved at the lower end of the market producing small, inexpensive copiers for small to medium-sized businesses. The company was set up in the mid-1960s and was highly successful for the first 12 years.

Towards the end of the 1970s, however, the company began to get into some difficulties as three of its competitors introduced new models which captured a significant proportion of its market. Copymatics tried to regain its market share by introducing, in 1981, a more advanced copier similar to those introduced by its major competitors. Although this met with some initial success, the company gradually lost ground again when it experienced problems meeting deadlines.

Various attempts were made by the management from the mid-1980s onwards to improve efficiency. None of these had any significant, positive effect on their market share, which generally continued to decline slowly over the next few years.

The Annual General Meeting

At the last Annual General Meeting the shareholders expressed concern about the situation and a small group of shareholders made an attempt to replace the Managing Director and two of the senior Directors. These three Directors only kept their positions by announcing that they had already instigated an internal investigation into the situation and that firm action would be taken as soon as the findings of the investigation were known.

The report on the investigation

The report of the investigation was presented to the Directors four months later. The report's main recommendation was that considerable streamlining was required in administrative and control procedures. The Directors discussed the issue and decided that the computer ought to be upgraded and a system introduced which would greatly improve the manufacturing control process and provide integration with a sophisticated office information system. This would not only improve the control of the manufacturing system but would also enable information to be relayed to the administration which would improve the speed and efficiency of the order processing.

The system implementation

The Directors called in the Data Processing Manager and asked him to co-ordinate the system implementation and change. When this news reached the Head of Administration he was angry and felt that he had suffered a loss of face in front of his staff. He recognised the need for change but considered that this was just another sign of favouritism. This was because the Data Processing Manager, who had been one of his assistants a number of years ago and with whom he did not get on, regularly played golf with the Managing Director.

The Data Processing Manager was enthusiastic about the new system and the challenge of the responsibility now being placed on him. He spent a lot of time with the computer suppliers discussing the potential system design. One outcome of this was that he realised the success of the implementation would be greatly assisted if there was a reorganisation of the work of three departments and a restructuring to create two departments instead of three.

He contacted the Managing Director and told him of the necessity for such change, suggesting that priority should be given to selecting some of the current clerical/secretarial staff for training. This would get them "up the learning curve" so that they would be able to adapt to the more demanding and responsible jobs when the new system was implemented. He also pointed out that firm control and regular monitoring would be necessary to identify and eliminate any weak points in the system. He suggested that the Head of Administration might share the load of this task with him. The Managing Director was somewhat apprehensive about such radical plans, particularly in view of the well-known antagonism between the Data Processing Manager and the Head of

Administration but, remembering his promise to the shareholders plus his determination to improve the organisation's market share, he rather reluctantly agreed to the plans.

Staff consultation plans

Recognising that certain rumours were already circulating throughout the company, the Managing Director decided that he had better call a meeting of staff in the three departments likely to be involved in restructuring. He would tell them something about the plans and reassure them that the new system would bring benefits to all and would result in improved career prospects for a number of them.

The day before the staff meeting, he called in the trade union officials to brief them on the plans. They stated that they were concerned about the situation and that they would be consulting with their members to decide what action would require to be taken.

Staff meeting

At the staff meeting the Managing Director was faced with considerable hostility and was asked several times for details of exactly what was planned and how this would affect staff. He was very irritated at the attitude of some of the workforce and on a number of issues gave only general answers. As he explained, this was either because it was much too early to be able to predict in such detail what would happen or because the issue was one which was a management affair and would not directly concern them. He himself was further concerned and angered by one or two awkward questions posed by the Marketing Manager, as he felt this was no time to show division among the management.

Selection of staff for upgrading

In order to show goodwill and to keep the unions happy, the management decided to offer a bonus to the staff selected to undertake the more demanding and responsible jobs which had been identified by the Data Processing Manager. In addition, management promised to review the status of the jobs once the new system was implemented. Information about the new jobs was sent to those clerical staff who were under the age of 50 in the three departments. Any of them who were interested in being considered for the new posts were asked to contact the Personnel Officer. An interview and selection process was subsequently carried out and staff appointed to the posts. It was very noticeable that the successful applicants were mainly in the younger age group, with only one of them being over 40 years of age. The management justified the decision by saying that the younger women all had better qualifications and that they were, in any case, more flexible and would be better able to cope with the added pressures and responsibilities.

Implementation

It was decided to introduce the changes in two phases. The first of these was the introduction of the new computer system, and appropriate training programmes were held for all staff who would use the new system. Departmental restructuring was to be left to phase two.

Management expected "teething" problems following the implementation of the system but were disappointed when these did not seem to disappear and others started to arise. The Data Processing Manager found it difficult to monitor the situation properly since so much of his time was taken up in answering questions and dealing with minor problems which arose in all departments. He was also very irritated by what appeared to be unhelpfulness on the part of the Head of Administration, although there was little to which he could point specifically.

It soon became clear that particular problems were occurring in the Marketing Department. Investigation highlighted that one of the senior staff was not co-operating with the demands of the new system and that the Marketing Manager was not prepared to force him to do so since he was a valued member of staff who was due to retire shortly. In addition, confusion had arisen because some other members of the department had not been made fully aware of the new procedures.

Problems also occurred in the three departments due for restructuring. As far as possible the staff occupying the new posts had been grouped together in one section of each department. In the past few weeks two of them had been complaining of headaches and one was experiencing pain in her arms and neck.

A number of the other staff whose terminals had been moved to allow for the regrouping were now complaining of glare. Some of them, along with two of the Secretaries, were annoyed that they had not been given the opportunity to apply for the new posts, while three of the others were bitter that they had not been chosen for the posts. Ill-feeling had built up in the departments and some very unfortunate remarks had been made. There had also been a noticeable increase in the number of days lost through illness and other reasons in the three departments.

ACTION

1 Analyse the case study and identify the problems relating to the planning and management of change which exist in Copymatics plc.

2 Does the case study highlight any other problems which exist within the company?

3 Take the role of consultants called in to advise on the current situation and to recommend a course of action which should be followed. Work as a group and

make a verbal presentation of your findings to a management team led by the Managing Director.

Your presentation should:

- outline the problems
- identify the causes
- make recommendations on the course of action which management should now adopt

Your presentation should last approximately 10 minutes and should be supported by visual aids and hand-outs where appropriate.

SECTION 10
TUTOR GUIDELINES

The success of a case study or role-play session is dependent not only on the quality of the material in the case study but also on how well the students are prepared for the techniques and, where a classroom situation is involved, how competently the tutor manages that session.

This section is designed to provide guidelines for tutors on the use of case studies and role-play exercises as tools for individual study on the part of the students and also for group study in tutorials and seminars.

A natural development from using such learning techniques is to find an appropriate method of assessing them. This links in with the move, over the past few years, away from assessing solely by means of traditional, end-of-session written examinations. Some guidelines are therefore given in this section on how to approach the assessment of group case study and role-play exercises.

With the increasing emphasis on students learning by means of case studies and role-play exercises, there is a growing need for tutors to develop skill in the production of appropriate material. The final part of the section is devoted to guidelines on the writing of case studies and role-play exercises.

10.1 Suggestions for the management of case-study sessions

As stated in Section 1, students initially find case studies often difficult and sometimes confusing. Training in case study technique is therefore vital. Once students feel comfortable with the technique they generally find case studies interesting and they usually enjoy the opportunity for group discussions, particularly where the dynamics among the group members are good.

The following are some suggestions for the management of classroom case study sessions:

- Before beginning the session, make sure that the students have an understanding of case study techniques. This is very often best carried out in an earlier session at the time when the case study is being distributed. It is also important during this session to make sure that the students are quite clear as to what it is that they are required to do.

- Preparation by the students *before* the case study session is not absolutely vital but does make for more efficient use of the session since time is then not spent reading and analysing the case. In preparation, students should be encouraged to follow through stages 1-9 given under *Guidelines for approaching a case study* in Section 1.2.

- The advantage of good preparation is that the student has thought about the case, related it to relevant theoretical knowledge and personal experience, and decided on some points and "answers" which can be put forward in the group discussion sessions. Subsequent group discussions then tend to be more lively and knowledgeable, which increases the value obtained by the student from the case study.

Group case studies

1 Divide the students into small groups. A group size of three or four is ideal. Groups of six or more tend to be less effective as there is less time for each group member to contribute and the likelihood of one or two members dominating the group is increased. With large group sizes it is also easier for a group member to make little or no contribution.

2 Ask each group to appoint a group reporter to give the group's feedback and findings at the end of the session. Over a series of case studies, it is advisable for everyone to have the opportunity to be a group reporter.

3 Encourage the groups to be realistic in their plans and not to go "overboard", to be detailed and practical in their recommendations and to

look for a relationship to their own experiences or ones which they recognise.

4 Allow the groups a short time to get started and then go round the groups as a "fly on the wall" to ensure that they are on the right lines. If they experience real difficulties or are on the wrong track, prompt them. Sometimes it is helpful to continue circulating round the groups for the duration of the discussion, while at other times it is not - particularly if the tutor finds it difficult not to monopolise the conversation or over-direct a group's thinking.

5 Make sure that sufficient time is left for feedback and discussion - it usually takes more time than you think. (About 30-40 minutes out of a two-hour session may be required for feedback.)

6 Use what system you like when the groups are giving their feedback. Some examples are given below:

- One group representative gives the complete group report. Subsequent group representatives, in turn, then give their complete reports. Overhead transparencies can assist in this type of feedback. This method is particularly useful where the solution is a package of measures.

- A similar procedure can be adopted but with each group representative reporting on the group's answer to one question before moving on to report on the next question.

- One group representative can present that group's report on the first question, often followed by general discussion and comment. Another group can then be asked to present the answer to the second question, and so on.

- Each group prepares a report but only one group is subsequently chosen to present its report, while the other groups comment on it.

Ensure that sufficient time is left for you as tutor to make comment where necessary, either at the end or after each report and discussion.

Remember:
There is usually no *one* right answer to the case questions. The validity of an answer is whether or not it is sensible, practical and likely to bring about a satisfactory result.

10.2 Suggestions for the management of role-play sessions

Role-play exercises are similar to case studies in that their success depends on the quality of the material, how well the students understand the technique and how much preparation they have undertaken.

A role-play exercise is often an extension of a case study where each student or group of students is required to adopt a role based on information given in the case. In one type of role-play the students are *all* given the same information and individuals or groups subsequently present their role-play after carrying out the instructions given in the case. (For example, information is presented in the case study about a particular problem situation within a company. Individual students or groups of students are required to take the role of Consultants called in by the company to analyse the situation, present a report to a management team on their findings and give their recommendations for "solving" the problem situation.) In this type of role-play individuals and groups are not interacting with each other and in most instances there is no element of competition.

A second type of role-play does involve interaction and, in many cases, competition between individuals or groups. It is common in such exercises for some information to be given to all the participants while other information is made available only to one team or to an individual to whom a specific role is assigned. In such instances it is vital that students do not divulge restricted information to other groups or individuals.

Guidelines

1 When running a role-play exercise, allow plenty of time for the students to prepare for the role. Where the exercise is a group exercise, time must also be allowed for the members of the group to meet to discuss the content and the presentational details.

Encourage students to have a "trial run" of any verbal presentation to enable them to test the mechanics of the presentation and, where important, the timing. Where a group has more than one presenter, the links between the presenters and the unity of the overall presentation should be examined. It is important that the group presentation appears to the audience as *one* presentation with several contributors rather than two or three different presentations.

In preparation for verbal presentations, students should be encouraged to pay attention to their presentational skills, eg clarity of expression, eye contact with the audience, use of visual aids.

In a role-play such as a negotiation exercise, it is *vital* for the students, particularly when working as a team, to discuss the strategy and tactics they hope to adopt. It is also vital for them to discuss their response to any foreseeable questions, answers, comments and tactics of the other team. In addition, they should discuss how they would respond if their "plan of campaign" becomes impractical or invalid as a result of new information (which was obviously in the other team's confidential brief) being presented to them during the negotiation itself.

Inexperienced students often find it difficult to prepare for all likely eventualities. They tend to assume that the other team will more or less follow one or perhaps one of two possible courses of action. They do not plan how they might react to the unexpected.

2 Meet with the students at some point during the preparation to ensure that they are preparing properly - they often tend to under-prepare and only realise this when running the exercise - but guard against influencing the direction or outcome of the role-play by imposing your ideas. Check that students are planning to play the role in keeping with the information which has been given to them.

3 Make sure that the students realise that, whereas they may well have to supply some additional information before and during the exercise, they must not get "carried away" and must certainly make any addition fit in with the information or type of role(s) assigned to them. Any additional information *must not* contradict any given information.

4 It is normal for a time limit to be set when running the role-play. Remember that it is not vital, nor even often desirable, for the students to feel that they must have reached the "end" of the exercise by that time. It is better that the exercise progresses at a natural speed and that the students get the experience of the events and pressures as they develop naturally, than that a false ending is imposed. Students in that situation will lose interest in the exercise and the learning will be reduced.

5 Run the exercise. The use of video equipment is very helpful to role-play exercises, particularly for the debriefing session.

6 During the running of some exercises, where there is potentially a confrontational aspect, you may have to intervene occasionally to break a prolonged stalemate situation. Make sure that your intervention is appropriate in the first place and that you do not over-direct the subsequent play by suggesting or imposing too many of your own ideas.

7 In a role-play exercise, one of the most important aspects is the debriefing:

- Ask the various participants for their reactions to the role play.

    eg Did they think it went well and if not, why not?
    Did they enjoy the exercise?

- Ask the observers for their reactions.

- Ask each team to assess its performance as a team and the performances of the members of that team.

    eg Did they behave as a team?
        Did they present a unified front?
        Did the team-leader lead and direct the team or did someone else take over the role?
        Did other members take their assigned roles?
        Did everyone make an appropriate contribution?
        Were there occasions when several members all spoke at once?

- Check whether or not there is agreement on what happened and what were the final decisions.

- Get the students to analyse the causes of behaviour.

- Get the different players to analyse how they felt during the exercise.

- Try to get the students to draw some conclusions about the way people behave.

- Get the students to comment on what could have been done to improve the running or the outcome of the exercise.

- Get the students to identify any other lessons they have learned from the role-play and draw overall conclusions.

- Plan any follow-up action (perhaps a re-run of the same role-play or a different one).

10.3 Assessing group case studies and role-play exercises

With so much student time and effort being devoted to group work, there is a growing desire to find acceptable methods of group assessment. Group assessment can be for written or practical work and it is with the practical work that many of the more exciting methods are associated.

Form of mark to be awarded

When assessing a group, one of the first decisions to be made is the basis on which the mark is to be awarded. This can take various forms, some examples of which are:

a   A mark is awarded to the group and this mark is subsequently recorded for each member of that group.

b   Individuals in the group are awarded a different mark, depending on their contribution to the group submission. This method depends on it being possible to assess each individual's contribution.

c   A combination of the above two methods is used where an individual's mark consists of two parts. One part is the common mark awarded to each member of the group and the second part is an assessment of the individual's contribution. The sum of the two parts gives the total mark for the individual.

d   A mark is awarded to the group as a whole and subsequently divided among the members. The mark may or may not be divided equally among the members of the group.

There are advantages and disadvantages in each of these four methods. Before any can be applied, it is important that each group makes a statement about the extent and the level of the contribution which the different members of the group have made. A written statement by the group on the division of work can be required to be submitted along with the group work itself.

Turning to the advantages and disadvantages of each of the four methods, it can be said that *a* is the simplest. There is no necessity to attempt to assess each individual's contribution and disputes over an individual's mark are rare since all group members are awarded the same mark. At the same time, the lack of any differentiation among group members can be a source of annoyance to those who feel that their contribution was substantially greater than that of others in the group, or who feel that the value of their contribution was reduced by the poor contribution of one member of the group.

Method *b* overcomes this problem by awarding individual marks. The difficulty occurs in that it is often impossible to distinguish one individual's contribution from that of the others. The more easily individual contributions can be identified, the less of a "group" submission it tends to become.

Method *c* tries to take the best of methods *a* and *b*. However, it, too, can be said to have the disadvantages of both - if to a lesser extent than either.

Method *d* is, in some ways, the most ambitious of the four methods. It has two advantages. It assesses the submission as a whole and yet allows total flexibility in the division of that mark among the members. This latter "advantage" can be more apparent than real if it becomes the norm for the mark merely to be divided equally among the members. It must be said also that method *d* has most scope for dissention among the group where there is a differentiation in the marks awarded to the different members.

Who assesses?

A second decision which has to be made is who is going to carry out the assessment.

1 The traditional method is for the tutor to undertake the assessment but it is quite usual nowadays for others to be involved. Where the group submission takes the form of role-play it is common for more than one person to undertake the assessment. A small panel can be formed from tutors or from representatives from business (often along with a tutor). Sometimes a student from a later year of the course, or a later year of another course, can be a member of the assessment panel. This is good personal development for that student.

2 One of the most ambitious schemes involves the students themselves, or students from other groups, being involved in the assessment. There is much to be said for such involvement as it develops within the students the ability to assess and to self-assess. It must also be remembered that tutors are not always aware of *all* the factors involved in the students' submission nor are they infallible, and discussion with the students about the mark to be awarded can often bring to light some aspect which causes the tutor to revise the mark.

3 Where a student is only one party to the assessment process, negotiation can be required - this is a very useful "life skill" for students to develop. Being part of the assessment process undoubtedly puts pressures on the students. It can, however, be very good for the students to experience such stresses and strains - particularly when "hard" decisions have to be made. It is normal for the tutor to have the final say on the mark which is awarded and to act as arbiter if disagreements arise.

4 When a composite mark is awarded for the group, it subsequently has to be divided among the members. This can be done by the tutor(s) or by the students themselves. There is considerable value in requiring the group to allocate the mark among the members. A major advantage of such a system is that it forces the group to undertake analysis and evaluation of the different

contributions. To do this effectively requires a considerable level of maturity in the students. The development of such an ability, however, is again a "life skill" much to be valued. The more important the mark is in terms of the students' overall assessment, however, the greater is the pressure on the group merely to divide the mark equally among the members and it is certainly common for groups, on the first few times that they are required to divide the mark, to indicate that the mark should be divided equally.

A commonly-held viewpoint among tutors who have no experience of students assessing themselves is that the students will "over-estimate" their mark. This does not tend to happen when students take the assessment seriously. In most cases students, when well prepared, react very responsibly and are more likely to under-value than over-value their submission.

Encouraging students to assess themselves is time-consuming as the tutor requires to discuss in detail with the students how they arrived at the mark they awarded themselves. Where there is a discrepancy between the mark the students awarded themselves and the mark the tutor would have awarded them, negotiation often requires to take place. It is important always to recognise and remember that the system of students making a contribution to their assessment only has validity and credibility where they *are* allowed to make a contribution. If the tutor is never prepared to reconsider his/her mark in the light of the students' comments, students will lose faith in the system, consider it a waste of valuable time and become disgruntled.

Where there *has* been over-valuing by the students, however, it is often because they have not recognised a "fault" or an "omission". When this is pointed out to them, and appropriate discussion has taken place, they are usually quite prepared to accept a reduction in their assessment. Occasionally it proves impossible to reach agreement over the mark. When this happens the tutor normally has the final say over what the mark should be.

Criteria for assessment

It is helpful for students to be given the criteria for assessment in advance of the submission of the work. Students are then aware of the relative importance of the different criteria, which enables them to prepare accordingly. It is of course vital for students to be given the detailed criteria if they have to take part in the assessment.

10.4 Writing a case study or role-play exercise

Tutors are often required to write their own case studies or role-play exercises. The following are some guidelines which might prove helpful.

1 Decide on the general problem area to be studied.

2 Decide on the objectives of the case study or role-play exercise.

3 Identify the various points that should be brought out by the case study or role-play exercise.

4 Briefly draft a situation which covers each point.

5 Identify a scenario for the case study or role-play exercise.

- The scenario must be realistic - though slightly exaggerated. It may contain more problems than normally would be found in a single, real-life situation. Each problem, however, should be realistic.

- The scenario must be within the understanding of the students.

- There are advantages in not using an actual case.

   eg Students can feel less threatened and defensive and therefore can look at the situation more objectively.

   There is less likelihood of the issues becoming clouded by extraneous irrelevancies.

- Identify the characters in the case study or role-play exercise and their relationships with each other.

- Avoid stereotyped characters and humorous names.

6 Write a short draft introduction setting the scene. This develops and clarifies the scenario. In some instances it is helpful to produce an organisational chart.

7 Take the draft situations written for step 4 above and relate them to the scenario created, making sure that the actions are consistent with the pattern of behaviour being developed for the relevant character(s).

8 Make sure that complexity is built in, where appropriate, and that some of the problems are hidden within the descriptions of the characters and their actions.

9   Try to write the case in a factual and unbiased style. Avoid statements which imply comment or criticism unless this is an essential and intentional part of the case.

10 Make sure that the case gives a correct impression of the passage of time.

11 Write the case as a narrative, linking together the various points and trying to create an interesting plot.

12 Make sure that instructions are clear.

Writing style

1   In general, use the past tense for the body of the case description. The present tense is often used for the immediate events leading to the decision which the students have to make.

2   Avoid the use of unusual and unknown terms.

3   Avoid the passive tense which can lead to monotony and clumsy sentences.

4   Avoid double negatives.

5   Break up the text by intelligent use of paragraphs and headings.

6   Avoid over-long and complex sentence construction.

7   Check for consistency of tenses, flow of language, accuracy of grammar and spelling, clarity of thought and logic.

Written specifically for SCOTVEC students ...

A Modular Approach to Text Processing Book 1
Ann Hackston, SCOTVEC Moderator and Senior Lecturer, Central College, Glasgow
Florence Ramage, SCOTVEC Moderator and Senior Lecturer, Motherwell College of Further Education
Consultant Editor: Margot Beynon, Curriculum Development Officer and SCOTVEC Senior Moderator

This text has been written to help teachers to meet the major changes in the SCOTVEC curriculum. It provides activity-based assignment material which is related to evaluation and assessment within the text processing modular scheme. It gives a carefully selected and interesting set of exemplar material. Tutors will find this useful when looking for assignments designed to meet the SCOTVEC requirements for Text Processing Modules 1-3.

ISBN 0-273-03322-0

A Modular Approach to Text Processing Book 2
2nd edition

This new edition addresses the structure of awards in Text Processing 4 and 5 from September 1991. There is no teaching strategy within this text as the aim is purely to provide assessment material to be used by the tutor in a flexible and open way.

ISBN 0-273-03887-7

Using Information Technology in Business
A Modular Approach
Elizabeth Rae, Lecturer at Central College of Commerce, Glasgow

The training material and assignments have been designed for the SCOTVEC Higher National Unit Level 3 Using Information Technology in Business but it is also suitable for SCOTVEC Computer Applications modular courses in Spreadsheets, Databases and Word Processing and for RSA, PEI and LCCI courses.

The book is divided into four sections:

- Word Processing
- Desktop Publishing
- Spreadsheets
- Databases

each section offering a complete range of activity-based learning assignments.

- A summary of commands is given at the beginning of each section for ease of reference.
- Solutions to the assignments are given at the end of each section.

The material is also suitable for use in an Open Learning environment.

ISBN 0-273-03726-9

Other titles on Administrative Management ...

Modern Business Administration
5th edition
Robert C Appleby, Development Officer, Worcester Technical College

Recommended on a wide range of administration courses, this book presents a readable account of business administration and management. The new edition includes information on management competences, international management and international business (with examples from throughout Europe), entrepreneurship, the management of information systems, just in time (JIT) and materials requirement planning (MRP).

This book is on the reading list of most accounting, secretarial and professional management associations. BTEC, SCOTVEC, HND business and finance students, and NEBSM students will find it useful. This 5th edition is accompanied by a Lecturer's Guide.

ISBN 0-273-03332-8

Modern Business Administration Lecturer's Guide
5th edition
Robert C Appleby
ISBN 0-273-03333-6

M + E
Management
Roger Bennett, Management Consultant

A fresh and lively text which gives full coverage of management syllabuses. It offers immediate access to the essential information on this subject, including developments such as networking, honeycomb structures, JIT and inventory systems. Examination questions are given as end-of-chapter progress tests and a comprehensive glossary is also provided.

Written for the management elements of business studies and professional courses such as the ACCA 2.5B Effective Management syllabus.

ISBN 0-7121-1421-1

Business Administration
Josephine Shaw, Training Consultant for Management and Support Services

This book provides an excellent introduction to the techniques of administration essential for any organisation to function efficiently. It focusses on the main systems and procedures of administration, such as data processing, filing systems, telecommunications and reprographics, together with the management of human resources and basic organisation theory.

Each chapter includes chapter objectives, a summary, self-assessment questions and more extensive assignments to aid students' comprehension of the text and extend their understanding of the subject.

The book will be essential reading for students taking the AAT Preliminary Certificate in Accounting, and an excellent introduction for the business administration parts of ICSA, IAM, IPS and other professional courses.

ISBN 0-273-03213-5

Management Appreciation
An Essential Handbook
Helen Harding, Lancashire Polytechnic

This compact and readable book covers the theory and practice of modern management and is essential reading for students studying management theory and practice as an integral part of a range of diploma, degree, professional and post-experience programmes. It provides a fascinating introduction to a wide range of contemporary management issues and is designed to give an awareness of the key issues and to act as a signpost to further reading.

ISBN 0-273-02268-7

Managing Technology for Competitive Advantage
Brian Twiss, Management Consultant in Technology Management and Forecasting
Mark Goodridge, Managing Director, Employment Consultants

"... for those who are involved in manufacturing industry and who have not thought through the problems that a changing environment poses and its impact upon the organisation ... then this book is required reading. I recommend it." Journal of Operational Research Society

ISBN 0-273-02955-X

Managing Change
A Strategic Approach to Organisational Development and Renewal
Bernard Burnes, Research Officer, Manchester School of Management, UMIST

One of the key attributes of successful companies in the 1990s will be their ability to identify the need for and manage the process of organisational change. The primary aim of this book is to provide management students and practising managers with an understanding of and a guide to effectively managing the complexities of organisational change. Written for degree courses and DMS, MBA and diploma in Business Administration students, the book may be used for courses on the management of change or as part of a course on organisational behaviour or human resource management.

ISBN 0-273-03376-X

M + E
Company Secretarial Practice
8th edition
George Thom, Tutor in Law, The Financial Training Company and Examiner for AAT Business Law, LCCI Commercial Law and IComA Law Relating to Business and Company Law

This M + E Handbook provides a knowledge of the application of English statutory provisions and Stock Exchange regulations and practice to the work of the company secretary, including the administrative procedures involved.

The new edition has been completely updated to cover the new ICSA syllabus, and to incorporate the Companies Act 1989, changes in Stock Exchange practice and the increased emphasis on financial services and their regulation. It is a book for students of the ICSA and those taking company law courses of CIMA and ACCA, practitioners and those involved in company administration, including company registrars, who require a knowledge of the English law. It also covers much of the ICSA's Certificate in Company Secretarial and Share Registration Practice.

ISBN 0-7121-0839-4